The Primary Teacher in Action

A look at the research literature

Deanne Boydell

Open Books

London

First published 1978 by Open Books Publishing Ltd,
11 Goodwin's Court, London WC2N 4LB

© Deanne Boydell 1978

Hardback ISBN 0 7291 0177 0
Paperback ISBN 0 7291 0182 7

British Library Cataloguing in Publication Data

Boydell, Deanne
    The primary teacher in action.
    1. Education, Elementary — Research
    I. Title
    372'.07'2   LB1028

ISBN 0-7291-0177-0
ISBN 0-7291-0182-7   Pbk

Set by Preface Ltd, Salisbury, Wiltshire
Printed and bound by Biddles Ltd, Guildford, Surrey

Contents

For Bill and John

Acknowledgements

The preparation of this book has been helped, in all its stages, by the efforts of various people. I should particularly like to thank my husband for his comments on the early drafts and Enid Jefferies for typing the manuscript.

An acknowledgement is also due to the Editor of *Education 3-13*. Chapter 4 is based in part on material originally published as 'Individual attention: the child's eye view' in *Education 3-13*, volume three, number one, April 1975, pp. 9-13.

1

Introduction

No-one would deny that the nature of British primary education has undergone a dramatic change. Over the past fifteen years or so new ideas and trends have resulted in the partial disappearance of the traditional type of classroom with its rows of desks arrayed before the teacher and a blackboard, all occupied by quiet, immobile children engaged in more or less identical tasks. Nowadays there is a vast collection of different techniques and philosophies, manifested not only in school buildings and classroom organisation but in methods and curricula and teachers' attitudes and relationships to children. Gone is the period when a student teacher would be castigated by her tutor because at one point during the lesson one of her charges 'was not looking at her'. Today's teacher is much more likely to be pulled up for failing to attend to a particular child rather than the other way round!

The forces underlying these shifts in outlook and approach are not fully understood although factors like disillusionment with the eleven-plus and streaming undoubtedly played some part. In

addition educational thinking stemming from the
work of reformers like Dewey and psychologists
such as Piaget contributed to a climate which was
conducive to change and enabled certain local education authorities (L.E.A.s) and individual heads and
teachers to play key innovatory roles in spreading
and implementing new ideas and practices. The
Plowden Report, published in 1967, gave voice to
the new outlook and became an added stimulus to
innovation in its own right. It was produced in
response to a directive from the then Minister of
Education, Sir Edward Boyle, who in 1963 asked the
Central Advisory Council for Education (England)
'to consider primary education in all its aspects, and
the transition to secondary education'. Three years
later the committee, under the chairmanship of
Lady Plowden, reported and their findings were
published the following year. The Report ran to two
volumes and over a thousand pages but its spirit and
underlying message is emblazoned on its cover in
the five simple words which make up its title,
Children and their Primary Schools. The reader
need go no further than the ninth paragraph to gain
some idea of what the authors have in mind: 'At the
heart of the educational process lies the child. No
advances in policy, no acquisitions of new equipment have their desired effect unless they are in
harmony with the nature of the child, unless they are
fundamentally acceptable to him' (para. 9).

Now, a decade later, our primary schools are once
again in the news but this time the reports are not
concerned with catching the enthusiasm of those
early innovators nor with the floods of foreign
visitors who have come to our shores to visit schools

all over the country. Neither do they focus on un-sensational portrayals of what school is really like for the vast majority of pupils. Instead, coming in the aftermath of the William Tyndale affair, they tend to have a somewhat sombre tone, narrowing attention to issues like standards in the basic skills and fuelling the controversy on traditional versus progressive methods. More and more people seem to be entering the debate. For good or ill there is an increasing expectation from outside the profession (as well as from certain quarters within) that primary teachers be accountable for what they do to the community as a whole.

The teacher has two options in the face of this more broadly based interest and concern in what she does. She can either offer passive resistance and shelter behind her long-established tradition of professional autonomy in the hope that the pressure will eventually abate. Alternatively she can take up the challenge and attempt to explain more fully to herself, her colleagues and the public at large what she believes, why she believes it and how all this relates to the way she operates in the classroom. Whilst the former option has obvious attractions for the teacher, with more than enough on her hands already, it carries a great danger. If teachers fail to enter and influence the debate, on both an individual and collective basis, decisions of great educational importance may be taken by those less qualified to make them, with disastrous conse-quences for teachers and children alike. If, on the other hand, the teacher can argue the case for what she does and why she does it, she may not only generate some kind of informed understanding with parents, employers and other interested parties but may further her own professional development in the process. This, in the long term, is much more likely to enhance her professional status and autonomy.

The underlying theme of this book is that the teacher owes it to herself and the community to take every available opportunity to further her own professional development. This, amongst other things, means taking constant critical looks at what she is doing in the classroom with a view to continually improving her style and monitoring and incorporating new experiences, insights and information. It does not mean jumping on to every new educational bandwagon; on the contrary, a self-critical outlook should go hand in hand with a high measure of intellectual autonomy and an ability to stand back and make rational judgements on new or controversial ideas and evidence in the light of personal experience. The teacher will be bombarded with the opinions, impressions and findings of others. Somehow or other she has to select and weave together what she finds important and relevant to the task in hand and create a coherent basis for action. This, of course, is only feasible in the context of experience: theoretical ideas and classroom practice are inextricably bound up with each other.

How can the social scientist help the teacher in this enterprise? To put the answer in a nutshell he can do at least two things: he can probe and try to explain the consequences of different teaching practices and he can document the various techniques and opinions which abound by investigating what other people do and think, thereby isolating the alternatives which already exist. Neither of these two activities are peculiar to the social scientist. As teachers go about their jobs they often work on hunches and are frequently on the look-out for the effects of their teaching and for the comments and views of other people. This indeed is one reason why teachers can and should play a much greater role in educational research than they usually do at present. However, the social scientist can, in addition, bring to any question a range of specialist techniques and focus singlemindedly on the task of investigation. The teacher just does not possess the time and energy to take on this extra work unaided, at least when she is actually teaching. Seen in this way, therefore, one of the social scientist's major jobs in educational research is to extend the teacher's knowledge and provide her with information which helps her evaluate what she is doing. The information may come in many different guises. It may stem from a national survey, a local investigation, an in-depth study of a single school or classroom. However, it is most unlikely that any given piece of information will be of equal interest to all teachers. It is therefore the researcher's job to provide enough background data about the schools, teachers and children in his study to enable each teacher to decide whether her situation is broadly similar and whether the study's findings and conclusions are relevant to her classroom.

At this stage it is necessary to emphasise one point: the teacher should not look to the researcher to provide definitive answers to controversial questions or to tell her how best to teach (although he may well make useful contributions to both these kinds of issues). The social scientist is not in a position to settle major disputes or tell the teacher how she should cope with a particular problem or handle a particular child. And this is not simply a reflection on the quantity and quality of research undertaken up to now. There are at least two major reasons why the social scientist should be regarded as an aide rather than an umpire on the one hand or an authoritative personal adviser on the other. In the first place all decisions about what should be done are at root value judgements, and this is so whether a national educational policy is under discussion or whether the teacher is pondering how to integrate a particularly awkward and anti-social child. It is not possible to argue directly from factual information to prescriptive statements without falling into the logical trap philosophers call the naturalistic fallacy. For example, the fact that primary teachers as a whole tend to put a relatively low emphasis on musical education does not necessitate any particular course of action (Ashton, Kneen, Davies and Holley, 1975). How the teacher responds to this item of information, indeed whether she responds at all, will depend very much on her values, on what she considers good and desirable. It is not possible to prove scientifically that any set of values is superior to another, although of course they are very much open to rational debate. The second reason for the teacher regarding the social scientist as an aide lies in the nature of his enquiries. He is concerned with generalisations and explanations of the recurring patterns he finds. There may be some special feature about a particular school, classroom or child which differentiates it from those studied and makes it an

exception to the general rule. The teachers concerned are the people most likely to know about
this.

This outlook on the use of research findings puts
the teacher in a key position. Not only must she
decide whether there is a match between her
situation and that studied but she must also go one
step further and evaluate whether the findings are
relevant to her. For instance, if she reads that
average, passive children may get neglected in
classrooms of the type she operates it would be
sensible for her to check that no child is inadvertently at risk with her system (Garner and Bing,
1973). This approach to the application of research
findings to the classroom makes special demands on
the social scientist as well. If part of his job is to help
the teacher decide on her own course of action by providing her with additional information and insights
which would be hard, if not impossible, for her to
come by on her own, then he must present his
findings in a way which is pertinent to the real issues
the teacher faces in the classroom. And it goes
without saying that they must be brought together
in an accessible form. The teacher cannot be
expected to spend hours rooting in libraries. The
question of disseminating research results is all-
important.

The psychologists, sociologists, anthropologists
and linguists currently engaged in educational
research embrace a wide range of outlooks and perspectives, not only in terms of their theories and
methods but also in how they regard their
professional roles. Few, however, would contest the
two main arguments outlined here. Firstly the

teacher should use research findings as she evaluates her thinking and her teaching (although there is considerable disagreement on which types of research are most relevant). Secondly the social scientist should refrain from telling the teacher what to do (although, once again, there are many opinions on what the teacher-researcher relationship should be). There would also be wide agreement amongst those engaged in research into primary education that their findings are beginning to raise some useful questions which deserve the attention of a wider audience.

The purpose of this book is to review recent work which has a bearing on some of the practical decisions with which the primary teacher is involved. A book of this kind is bound to be selective; it cannot include every piece of research ever undertaken in a primary school; nor can it cover an exhaustive list of the teacher's legitimate concerns. It focuses on five themes which are of widespread interest to teachers and on which the researcher has something useful to say. These are the teacher's aims, her style of classroom organisation, the consequences of individual attention, the implications of using groups, and the nature of the self-fulfilling prophecy. The criterion for the selection of studies described is eclectic: an investigation is reported whenever it contributes to the topic under discussion. In practice this means that a wide range of social scientific perspectives are represented and that there are references to many of the major pieces of investigation conducted in British primary school classrooms in the post-Plowden era. The emphasis in the second half of the book is on classroom research, that is to say on studies which have looked at classroom interaction, at what teachers and pupils actually do and say to each other during the natural flow of classroom events. Owing to the failure of previous methods to produce the hoped-for insights, observational work of this kind has become increasingly popular of late. Quite apart from its promise as a research tool it carries an obvious common sense appeal. If you want to find out more about teachers and pupils and the nature of classroom learning, surely the best place to be is in the classroom?

At first glance a chapter on aims, on what teachers are trying or intending to do, may seem a strange place to start an examination of the primary teacher in action. However, it is in line with the view that the commonly drawn distinction between thinking and action, between theory and practice, is not only artificial but also highly confusing: what a teacher does is influenced to some extent at least by what she thinks and the opinions and views she comes to hold will in part reflect her classroom experiences. Thinking is an integral part of teaching.

Lady Plowden has argued recently 'that despite day to day pressures and responsibilities the teachers in the schools should have time to clarify in their own minds what it is that they are trying to achieve' (Plowden, 1973). She believed that each teacher must go through three stages — first, the academic acceptance (without full responsibility for implementation) of 'best' primary school practice, second, a realistic interpretation of this within the school situation and third, a constant reconsideration of the philosophy behind day to day work involving the measurement of what each child was doing in the light of this philosophy. She was convinced that this third stage was vital to keep standards high and avoid stagnation of thinking. In addition she felt that this third stage was where the teacher should re-assess personal strengths and be aware of any weaknesses.

Although Lady Plowden considered that the three Rs remained as necessary as ever at the primary stage she argued that *what* is learnt is less important than *how* it is learnt and that what is learnt only becomes important as maturity is reached. This of course is not an argument for saying that anything goes in the primary school, far from it. For, as she contended, it is not sufficient to explain an approach by saying 'this is *what* we do'. It is necessary to go one step further and say 'this is *why* we do it'. If methods are adopted without the support of a coherent, underlying belief and realistic aims they may fail to achieve the quality of learning which can be reached. And she believed that further clarification of thinking was needed by teachers following more formal methods as well as those working in progressive schools: 'Time can be wasted by the boredom of being taught formally at the junior stage as well as by playing aimlessly with sand and water on first entry to school'.

Clearly the ability to put forward a coherent rationale for what you are doing is no guarantee whatsoever that you are effective in practice and perhaps this is one reason why there is such widespread scepticism and dissatisfaction with educational 'theory' and why 'theory' and 'practice' tend to be seen separately instead of as closely linked and interdependent. An informed understanding of what you are doing and why you are doing it is not enough; however, it is difficult to see how high-quality teaching can take place without it. To argue against the need for a rational approach to teaching is to suggest that teachers, and would-be teachers, can be treated as mindless automatons — hardly an attractive or viable proposition!

It is very easy for discussions on aims to get completely bogged down. Small wonder, because to answer the question, 'How should I teach?', the teacher needs to consider not only her experience and knowledge of education but her whole personal outlook to life as well. Chapter 2 takes up this question and brings together a number of studies which have looked at educators' opinions on what the aims of primary education should be. Its purpose is not prescriptive because an underlying tenet of this whole book is that the social scientist cannot tell the teacher what to do. Instead the chapter opens up and reviews some of the issues which concern and divide teachers and ends with a brief look at a fascinating piece of research into teachers' perceptions of the constraints and influences which affect what is actually taught in the primary school. It provides some interesting insights on the interface between aims and practice.

It is perhaps a paradox of the British educational system that the very same freedom which allows and encourages innovation and reform also protects teachers' rights to adhere to old-fashioned ideas and practices. Indeed, the coexistence of new and old approaches is almost inevitable in any system which permits teachers to hold the prime responsibility about how they should teach. In some cases teachers' feelings on this matter run so deep that they will move to another school in order to find an atmosphere which is more in line with their own sympathies, be they progressive or traditional. Often, however, differences of opinion about how children should be taught manifest themselves in a rich variety of ways within a single school. In some classrooms children might be taught quite tradition- ally whereas next-door, or across the corridor, they might be participating in a totally different style of educational experience. And it is obviously not an all-or-nothing affair: many classrooms reveal a mixture of strategies both old and new. The teacher's method of classroom organisation can provide many clues to how she teaches and this will even hold for a visitor who comes after school hours. How is the furniture arranged? What type of resources are on display? What does the timetable say about how children spend their time?

This emphasis on classroom organisation does not imply that organisational features constitute the sole criteria needed for assessing the existence or diffusion of new ideas. Nor does it imply that effective organisation is all that is needed for effective teaching. There is a great deal more to monitoring innovation and becoming a good teacher than a concern with classroom organisation. The teacher's relationship with her class as evidenced in her ongoing behaviour and attitudes is another realm which clearly warrants careful study. Nevertheless the teacher's organisational frame- work can provide useful pointers to her philosophy and methods.

Perhaps it is because organisational decisions are so much easier to describe and discuss than ideas about aims and objectives and curricula that definitions of the 'integrated day', a term which seems very old although it was not even mentioned in the Plowden Report, tends to be couched in organisational language. Brown and Precious (1968), for instance, defined the integrated day as 'a school day which is combined into a whole and has the minimum of timetabling'. Perhaps it is because of an understandable desire to translate complex and subtle thinking into concrete terms that educators have been only too keen to pin down new ideas into physical and organisational terms. In the U.S.A., for example, the identification of 'open education', that is to say education modelled broadly on informal Plowden-type infant school practice, with 'open-plan schools' led to commentators stressing that the two were not synonymous. Open education can take place in traditional buildings, however desirable purpose-built units might be. Conversely the existence of open-plan buildings is no guarantee that any form of open education is actually occurring inside them. The writer is reminded of one prestigious open-plan school she visited in the U.S.A. where one teacher had arranged her class in rows in one small corner of a vast hangar-like carpeted area designed for a hundred or so children. There is also an anecdote, probably exaggerated but nevertheless relevant, of the American principal who became convinced of the value of an informal approach and engineered an overnight removal of desks and chairs to force his staff to change their style. The results were disastrous. The moral is simple: the business of teaching is not reducible to manipulations of the physical environment and classroom organisation. Both play a role but it is problematic whether either holds the key.

Having sounded these warning notes about equating new ideas with physical and organisational changes it still seems pertinent to take a close look at what is known about teachers' techniques of classroom organisation. In the first place it is often a topic of great practical interest. It may not be something which the experienced teacher thinks very much about but, for the young teacher embarking on her career, or the established teacher facing pressures to alter her style, whether children sit in rows or groups, whether they have individual or group timetables, whether they have a subject-based or integrated approach to the curriculum, are unavoidable decisions. They epitomise her professional freedom, bring home her educational responsibilities to the children in her charge and provide visible evidence of her agreement or disagreement with the strategies of other members of staff. In the second place there is that hoary and recurring debate on the merits of traditional versus progressive methods. Whilst this controversy clearly runs much deeper than straightforward organisational decisions as to whether children should sit in groups or rows and be allowed to talk and move around the classroom or made to be quiet and sit still, the different approaches are generally characterised, at least partially, in organisational terms. Informal (or formal) techniques of organisation are not, by themselves, enough to guarantee informal (or formal)

types of classroom activities. In fact the Bullock
Report (1975) commented that changes in organisation within schools had not always been matched
by changes in classroom practice. However, organisational decisions can be of vital importance.
Chapter 3 examines the topic of classroom organisation in some detail. It starts with a brief look at
those frequently bandied terms 'family grouping'
and the 'integrated day'. It passes on to a review of
what, in organisational terms, is known about the
spread of innovation and ends with a critical look at
some of the lessons of the Bennett study (1976). This
classified teachers into different styles on the basis of
their answers to questions with a high organisational content in one section of a self-report
questionnaire. It attempted to investigate the
relationships between different teaching styles and
rates of pupil progress.

If organisation is to do with the provision of an
orderly structure or framework, teaching method is
a closely allied concept: it is possible to talk about
the methods for organising a classroom or school
day as well as about the organisation needed for
particular methods to be used. However, traditional
usage has tended to differentiate between the two
although they are closely related in practice.

Organisation is generally used to include such
things as the physical lay-out of the classroom, the
grouping of children, the provision of resources, the
planning of activities and the allocation of time to
different areas of learning. Although a teacher can
and does spend a considerable part of her classroom
time on these matters (Hilsum and Cane, 1971) it is
possible to envisage a classroom being so organised

that it could run successfully for some time (in the
sense that children would know what to do and how
to get on) with minimal teacher intervention.
Indeed, the teacher might not even be there for a
fairly long time. The same is certainly not true of
methods as conventionally understood, activities
like class teaching, providing private individual
attention and working with groups. Although each
method requires a suitable pre-arranged form of
organisational framework the teacher must be
physically present and interacting with children. A
teaching method, unlike an organisational strategy,
necessitates the teacher's presence and says something about her behaviour in the classrom.

Teaching methods, along with classroom
organisation, provide yet another perspective on the
teacher's aims, values and assumptions. This is one
reason why comparisons of different methods along
with comparisons of different organisational frame-
works, should be broad in outlook: to some extent at
least different methods and organisational strategies
are aiming at different things. Different approaches
are rarely introduced just because of hopes that they
will prove more efficient at reaching currently
valued objectives (although programmed and
computer-aided instruction are two possible exceptions). As often as not a great deal more is at stake,
ranging from hoped-for spin-offs in other directions
to major shifts in underlying values and opinions
about the nature of education itself. Individual attention, for instance, may be considered of paramount
importance in teaching reading and may be
advocated for this reason alone. However, during
his private time with the teacher the child is likely to

learn a great deal more than how to follow the adventures of Janet and John in print. How the teacher talks and looks and sits, along with the very act of being singled out for attention, either through his own initiative or the teacher's, will tell the child a great deal about the teacher's relationship to him. Some teachers would regard the quality of this relationship of equal or greater importance than the child's reading attainment. Regardless of whether or not this particular opinion is shared the teacher should always beware of any sweeping claims made about the merits or faults of any approach if the comparison is based on a restricted range of features (see Chapter 3).

One well-known aspect of modern classroom practice is the individualised approach. It was strongly recommended by the Plowden Report (1967) and underlies much of its thinking: 'any class, however homogeneous it seems, must always be treated as a body of children needing individual and different attention' (para. 75). Two exploratory surveys undertaken in this country have suggested that individual work has gained widespread approval (Bealing, 1972; Bennett, 1976). Although there is no comprehensive documentary evidence, it seems likely that the method of individual attention is also very popular. It is not at all difficult to imagine how many eyebrows would be raised if the words of one well-remembered teacher were uttered today: 'Go away little boy, I have no time for the individual'. No matter how out of line that particular *cri de coeur* from an earlier generation may be with modern sentiment, it sums up a very important issue: given a class of thirty or more how can any teacher, no matter how expert or how well-intentioned, give adequate personal attention to all her pupils? To pose this question is not to suggest that individual attention is a wrong approach but rather that it needs much more careful scrutiny than it is customarily accorded. Only in this way will its values and limitations be properly understood. All kinds of questions need to be asked. Do the same children receive the bulk of the attention for most of the time? Are some types of children more successful than others in gaining and holding the teacher's help? How can the effects of the inevitable low average amount of contact each child receives be ameliorated? Chapter 4 discusses these and other questions in the light of what various classroom investigations have discovered about the dynamics of classrooms run on a largely individualised basis.

Despite its emphasis on the needs of individual children the Plowden Report advised teachers to be flexible in their choice of approach and included group learning, with its implications for teaching methods and classroom organisation, among their many suggestions. It argued that 'groups of three to 15 pupils are good for many kinds of school work. In this way children learn to get along together, to help one another and realise their own strengths and weaknesses, as well as those of others' (para. 757). Is it really as simple as all that? The two surveys referred to in the previous paragraph reported that many teachers used group work; but they also found that it was not as popular as individual work. Could this be because of the problems of setting up work conditions which really do help children to 'get along together' (para. 757)? No-one can answer this question for sure, although there is sufficient evidence from exploratory studies to suggest that this might indeed be the case. The investigations have focused on many questions which teachers might legitimately ask. What really happens when children work in groups? Does the size of the group matter? Is the composition of any consequence? Do children interact very much with each other? Do they waste a lot of time? These and other issues are followed up in some detail in Chapter 5 which also takes a close look at the rationale for group learning.

The teacher's aims, her style of classroom organisation and her teaching methods are all closely bound up with each other and are all germane to the task of teaching. But what of the opportunities these provide for the teacher's relationships with children? What kinds of attitudes, expectations, values and ideas is the teacher transmitting, perhaps even unconsciously, within the framework she has established? To answer this question it is necessary to look very closely at the complexities of teacher-pupil exchanges and for this purpose it is absolutely vital for the researcher to spend a lot of time observing the teacher in action. It is possibly true to say that the educational researcher faces no greater challenge than increasing our understanding of the highly complex processes at work. It is also probably true to say that there is no other single area in which the teacher would more appreciate the researcher's involvement. It is, after all, this 'human' side to teaching which distinguishes the teacher from a computer, a television set or a teaching machine (although this is not to denigrate the wise use of these technological aids).

In 1968 a book reverberated around educational circles in the U.S.A. and caused a tremendous stir. Called *Pygmalion in the Classroom* it was a report of a study in which teachers were given false information about the latent potential of some of the children in their class (Rosenthal and Jacobson, 1968). These children, chosen at random, were designated as 'bloomers' and the results seemed to show that they did in fact 'bloom' as compared with groups of children of similar measured ability. It really did seem that when teachers expected children to achieve (even on the basis of incorrect information) they somehow communicated their aspirations and the children responded accordingly. The study has subsequently come in for a great deal of criticism on design grounds (there were statistical mistakes, logical flaws and so on) but the notion of the self-fulfilling prophecy remains firmly entrenched and has attracted a great deal of interest. After all, it accords with common sense: children are more likely to attain high standards if someone lets them know that quality work is expected. Moreover it is central to the issue of the teacher-pupil relationship: how does any child acquire goals and aspirations and pick up the teacher's opinions about his likelihood of attaining them? And finally there is the hope that it might help explain why children from low social class backgrounds often perform poorly at school.

Chapter 6 takes up this notion of the self-fulfilling prophecy with special reference to the contributions made by studies undertaken in British classrooms. Here, as in previous chapters, it will be noticed that the researcher's work is in its infancy, that many more questions are raised than answered. However, that is one of the purposes of research into teaching. The hope for the future must be that the teacher and researcher forge a relationship which is increasingly helpful to both. Researchers, as well as teachers, need the ability to be self-critical.

2
Aims

'What should I do?' It would be interesting to keep a log of the number of times a teacher asks herself that question in some form or other during the course of a day's work in the classroom. Should she let one group of children try out the new mathematics kit that has just been sent on trial? Should she tie Simon's shoelace again? Should she ignore Mark's fooling around on this particular occasion? Should she agree to Alison and Heather telling the class about the play they want to do? The list of decisions would be almost endless, ranging from matters the teacher regards as almost inconsequential to issues she rates of great importance.

Each time the teacher responds to that frequent and deceptively simple question, 'What should I do?', she invokes her own philosophy of education with its underlying aims and assumptions. It may have been acquired almost unconsciously during training or worked out with great soul-searching. It may be hazy in parts or even inconsistent. However, it is an integral part of her teaching: what the teacher does is inextricably linked to what she values, to what she regards as good and desirable. It may well be, of course, that the teacher cannot operate in the way she would ideally wish. Even so, the way she comes to terms with the circumstances in which she finds herself will again reflect her values, a point explored further at the end of this chapter. Moreover, unless the teacher is considered a mindless automaton the aims she holds are open to rational discussion. Indeed it is possible to go further and argue that they *should* be open to debate.

Gone is the period when there was so much agreement about the nature of education, and the teaching skills it entailed, that a consideration of aims, of what the teacher was intending or trying to do, could be safely (if unwisely) ignored. Today it is virtually impossible to neglect them. Whether she likes it or not the teacher is faced with a bewildering array of ideas and practices, many of which appear to conflict. And she finds this great diversity wherever she looks, to her colleagues, to the educational press or to the so-called specialists and experts. She lives, too, in a society where conflicting value systems exist side by side and almost everything seems open to question. It is against this background that she has to decide how she is going to teach and face the challenge posed by colleagues, perhaps even within her own school, who have different priorities and who disapprove of her approach. What she does with her new class on 5 September, when the new head arrives, may be a real issue in every sense of that word. Is she to press on as before, give full-hearted support to the ideas she knows the new head wants to encourage, or try to find some middle ground? By no stretch of the imagination is reflection on aims an optional extra for the philosophically inclined.

Although it is true to say that philosophical deliberations about aims are essential it is equally important to emphasise that philosophical analysis alone is insufficient when it comes to translating thoughts into actions. No matter how successfully the teacher articulates her own particular pedagogical standpoint there is no guarantee that she will deal appropriately with particular classroom situations. It may increase the chances of this happening and be a vital ingredient of high quality teaching, but that is all. Virtually everyone has come across that archetypal headmaster, renowned for his views on democratic procedures, respected and admired for his ability to put them across in public and loathed by his staff and pupils for his authoritarian and patronising manner. Words and actions can differ greatly. Deciding what to do, and then putting those ideas into practice, are probably the most challenging tasks facing any teacher. However, she is not alone in this enterprise. The educational researcher can help in several ways.

As explained earlier, in Chapter 1, the educational researcher can do at least two things. In the first place he can probe and investigate the consequences of different classroom practices. The teacher can then think about the implications of teaching in different ways with the benefit of objective information. In the second place he can describe and document different teaching techniques and collect other people's opinions on a scale which the teacher could not undertake herself. The teacher can then consider her own teaching in the light of existing ideas, some of which may be new to her.

There is a sense in which all the research described

in this book relates to aims, to the question of deciding what should be done. Aims are closely linked to practice: aims influence practice and practical experience influences aims. Aims should therefore always be considered along with the matters of classroom organisation, teaching methods and the teacher-pupil relationship, all of which are examined in the following chapters. The remainder of this chapter is concerned with setting the scene for this broadly based approach to deciding how to teach. It focuses on views about the aims of primary education and ends with a brief look at the constraints and influences which actually affect what is taught in primary schools.

The story begins with the Plowden Report (1967). Although the committee did not conduct a survey in the strict sense of the word they adopted a technique often employed by social scientists at the beginnings of their enquiries. They posed an open-ended question and asked their witnesses for their views on the aims of primary education. They found a wide general measure of agreement although they noted that 'many of the replies seemed to have as much relevance to other phases of education as to primary' (para. 497). This point has been reiterated by Dearden (1968) when he pointed out that 'there are no aims of *primary* education. There are only aims of education which are to be pursued in a manner appropriate to the primary *stage*.' Junior and infant school heads emphasised the all-round development of the individual and the acquisition of the basic skills necessary in contemporary society. Most were thinking of the three Rs although, as the committee pointed out, communication by the spoken word is at least as important as writing and for the majority perhaps even more important (a theme developed in the Bullock Report, *A Language for Life* (1975)). Many heads mentioned religious and moral development and some mentioned physical development and the acquisition of motor skills. Much use was made of phrases like 'whole personality', 'happy atmosphere', 'full and satisfying life', 'full development of powers', 'satisfaction of curiosity', 'confidence', 'perseverence' and 'alertness' (para. 497).

A recent survey in the north-west of England has also emphasised the importance primary teachers attach to the basic skills and to socio-emotional development (Bennett, 1976). Four hundred and sixty-eight fourth-year junior teachers rated each of nine aims on a five-point scale with respect to its importance to their class (not important, fairly important, important, very important, essential). By far and away the most important was 'The acquisition of basic skills in reading and number work' which was regarded as essential by 81 per cent of the sample. The aim perceived as next in importance to the basic skills was 'The acceptance of normal standards of behaviour' followed by 'Helping pupils to cooperate with each other', 'An understanding of the world in which pupils live', 'The enjoyment of school', 'The encouragement of self-expression' and 'The development of pupils' creative abilities'. Bottom of the list came 'Preparation for academic work in secondary school' and 'The promotion of a high level of academic attainment'.

How useful are general statements of aims like these and those put forward to the Plowden committee? Interestingly enough the Plowden

Report observed that some of the head teachers who were considered by H.M. Inspectors to be most successful practitioners were least able to state their aims in a clear and convincing way. Does this mean that practical statements of objectives would be more valuable? This was certainly the view of the authors of the Report who wrote that 'general statements of aims, even by those engaged in teaching, tend to be little more than expressions of benevolent aspiration. . . .' (para. 497). They were of the opinion 'that a pragmatic approach to the purposes of education was more likely to be more fruitful' (para. 501).

A fascinating investigation carried out by two researchers in the U.S.A. came to similar conclusions. They studied a so-called 'open education' programme in which teachers, with the help of advisers, were trying to implement the practices of innovatory British classrooms. The two investigators had the challenging task of translating the programme's underlying philosophy into terms which would have implications for assessment and research. Right from the start they were concerned with the communication gap which so often exists between researchers and practitioners and they consequently stressed very close cooperation with the teachers and advisers working on the programme: they attended teacher conferences and workshops, interviewed and accompanied advisers on school visits and spent a great deal of time participating in classroom life. The researchers found that although the people participating in the programme had great difficulties in stating objectives they had very strong convictions about the process of education, about how children should be taught. Accordingly the researchers focused on what the teacher did rather than on statements of specific objectives (Bussis and Chittenden, 1970).

The investigators found that ten recurrent themes seemed to sum up the open teacher's role. Two were concerned with the teacher's ideas, that is to say with her ideas about children and the process of learning and her ideas about herself as a person. The remaining eight were concerned with activities, with what the teacher should do when children were present and what she should do when they were not. One was *provisioning* the classroom with a wide variety of materials with an eye to their potential value in learning and to sensible practical arrangements for their use. A major goal of provisioning was to provide opportunities for children to choose and this led into a second theme. By engaging children in an activity which they value and find of interest and by becoming involved in what they do, the teacher should be able to *diagnose the learning* that is taking place through the feedback she obtains. This activity was closely related to a third, namely *guiding and extending learning,* and also formed the basis of a fourth, namely *reflective evaluation* of the children when they were not present. A fifth theme was that the teacher should *seek to promote her own personal growth,* for instance by sharing ideas and observations about children and learning with other teachers, getting to know the local community and following a hobby like music or photography. The three remaining features of the teacher's role focused on the quality of her classroom relationships. The first of these was a *respect for persons*, especially a respect for an activity or product as a legitimate expression of another person's interest even if the teacher did not share that interest herself. Next was a concern for *honesty of encounters*. This meant that the teacher should direct a child to another resource if she herself could not help, give children honest evaluations of their work tempered by judgements of the particular child and product in question and be realistic by setting obvious limits and rules to free choice and free expression where, for instance, a child was being destructive. Finally, as children may look to the teacher for help in handling a wide range of emotional experiences, the teacher should provide the *warmth* necessary in any relationship where one person is willing to depend on another.

As an aside it is interesting to note that two other American researchers followed up this work by looking at the writings of twenty-eight authors or co-authors with a view to finding out how much they emphasised these characteristics (Walberg and Thomas, 1971). There were sixteen open educators in the sample which included the Plowden Report (1967) and books and articles by Blackie (1967), Featherstone (1967) and Brown and Precious (1968), to name but some. The investigators slightly modified the original list of features and rated each author for each theme.

Obviously a survey of this kind is very limited and no substitute for reading the original works. Nevertheless it serves a useful purpose in pointing out the areas of general consensus. As the original list of characteristics emerged from an in-depth study of an open education programme it is hardly surprising that the sixteen open educators in the sample strongly emphasised most or all the themes. Much more interesting is the fact that instruction, conceived in terms of the guidance and extension of learning based on individual attention and involvement, the encouragement of independence and the exercise of real choice within a framework of long-term goals was stressed very strongly by all sixteen authors. It was the only theme to receive such unanimous heavy support. In addition fourteen of the group gave a similar heavy emphasis to the related theme of provisioning for learning, that is to say providing children with an appropriate range and richness of materials and conditions which maximise their ability to learn at their own rate in their own ways. Reflective evaluation of diagnostic information, although still obtaining moderate emphasis, received less attention than any other theme.

This analysis of the teacher's role as propounded by practitioners and as discussed in the literature, goes some way beyond the 'expressions of benevolent aspiration' mentioned in the Plowden Report (para. 497). It adds some flesh to the phrases they used and, by catching part of the flavour of innovatory practices, provides another perspective. However, its basis in a single experimental programme is narrow, its vocabulary is somewhat alien to British ears and its focus on teachers is rather one-sided. A recent survey carried out in this country serves as both a complement and a contrast to this American work. Funded by the Schools Council and based at the University of Birmingham School of Education it set out to examine the opinions of primary school teachers about the aims of primary education. Its basis was broad as opinions were gathered from a representative national sample using a questionnaire. Many teachers helped in the questionnaire's development and their influence is obvious. The questionnaire's format and language is straightforward and its focus is practical. When giving their views on aims respondents were asked to think about what children in the middle range of ability should have at the end of their primary education (Ashton, Kneen, Davies and Holley, 1975).

Begun in 1969 just two years after the publication of the Plowden Report, the research ran for over three years as a cooperative venture between a university-based research team and groups of teachers who met in various parts of the country. Their major product was a list of seventy-two aims and objectives (strictly speaking aims refer to general statements of purpose and objectives refer to more precise and narrow formulations). They ranged over three main areas. These were knowledge (e.g. 'The child should have an understanding of how his body works'), skills (e.g. 'The child should be able to read fluently and accurately at a minimum reading age of eleven') and qualities (e.g. 'The child should be industrious, persistent and conscientious'). They were concerned, moreover, with many aspects of development — intellectual, physical, aesthetic, spiritual/religious, emotional/personal and social/moral. These seventy-two aims formed the core of the questionnaire completed by 1,513 teachers in 201 schools in the national survey (three-quarters of the teachers approached).

How were these aims arrived at? No claim is made

for the list being either complete or exhaustive and the analysis of some of the early discussions provides some interesting insights (Davies and Ashton, 1975). It leads one to suspect that one of the most valuable aspects of the whole venture might have been the stimulus and opportunity it provided for the teachers participating in the project to engage in a critical evaluation of their own personal pedagogical standpoints. Indeed the second part of the project's brief was to devise techniques for thinking about aims which teachers could use for themselves (Ashton, Kneen, Davies and Holley, 1975). Initially seventy Midlands teachers were involved in writing and talking about the aims of primary education. Detailed analysis of what they wrote and spoke about led on in the second phase, when thirty-one more teacher groups from Devon, Dorset, Northumberland, Durham and north Yorkshire joined the original seven, to more focused discussions centring on twenty-four categories of aims identified during the first phase. In the third and final phase the thirty-eight groups worked to a structured brief, scrutinising and formulating aims with respect to a two-way classification system. The three areas of knowledge, skills and qualities mentioned in the previous paragraph formed one axis and the six listed aspects of development formed the other.

As the work progressed it became apparent that how teachers looked at aims was related to other issues. Fundamental beliefs about the whole purpose of education was one: is it primarily concerned with developing individual talents and interests (the individual view) or with equipping children with the skills and attitudes appropriate to the society in which they live (the societal view)? Different views about which aspects of children's development mattered most was another (intellectual, moral or some other?). Varying perceptions of their role as teachers was a third. Accordingly items probing these issues were included on the questionnaire used in the national survey.

The teacher questionnaire was divided into four sections. The first section collected background information about the teacher (sex, age, marital status and so on). The second section presented two statements about the purpose of education. One stressed the societal view and one the individual view and teachers were asked to allocate five points between the two statements to indicate the relative weight they would give to each. It also listed various aspects of the child's development and asked the teacher to indicate the two she considered most important and the two she considered least. The third section presented the seventy-two aims and objectives worked out by the teacher discussion groups. Teachers were asked to bear in mind the children in their own school who were in the middle range of ability and at the end of their primary education and to rate each aim on a five-point scale (utmost importance, major importance, important, minor importance, no importance) with the added option of saying it should not be an aim of primary education at all. The final section presented five short descriptions of the teacher's role, each reflecting a different approach to education, and the teachers were asked to indicate the extent to which they agreed with each one using another five-point

scale (strongly agree, agree, neither agree nor disagree, disagree, strongly disagree) and to pick out
the one description closest to their own personal
approach to education.

The survey collected a mammoth amount of data
about teachers' opinions which was processed by
computer. What did it reveal about the national
situation? With respect to the broad purposes of
primary education almost three-quarters of the
teachers balanced the two views — societal and
individual — as nearly as the instruction allowed
and of the remainder only about one in twenty opted
entirely for one view or the other. When it came to a
consideration of various aspects of children's
development there was rather less agreement with
only about half the teachers concurring about any
given one. However, emotional/personal,
intellectual and social development emerged as
generally the most important, aesthetic, physical
and spiritual/religious development as the least,
with moral development coming in between. At
least two teachers in five agreed or strongly agreed
with each of the five roles and, interestingly enough,
the two which picked up the most disagreement
were the two extremes — the most traditional and
the most progressive. A similar picture of modera-
tion came out when teachers indicated their own
approach: almost half opted for the moderate role,
about one fifth opted for the traditional and progressive role descriptions and the remainder split almost
equally between the most traditional and most
progressive roles.

The overwhelming majority of teachers thought
all of the seventy-two aims were important. They

gave precisely half the aims an average rating which approached utmost or major importance. Amongst these thirty-six aims, three major emphases were detected. One concerned the child's personal development and it seemed to consist of three strands. One strand was a general sense of well-being and positive orientation towards school (coupled to a positive and purposeful approach to out-of-school leisure activities), the second strand was a sense of assurance and competence and the third strand concerned the development of individuality. The second priority area focused on social and moral development. The child was required to learn socially acceptable behaviour based on a growing awareness of moral values and to have a positive, kindly and confident involvement in social relationships. The basic skills formed a third priority area, with the emphasis coming first on reading, then on oracy and finally on mathematics. These findings are very much in accord with the results mentioned earlier in this chapter (Plowden Report, 1967; Bennett, 1976).

Perhaps more interesting still are the aims which were not among the thirty-six priority aims. Completely excluded from the top half of the list which put the aims in order of importance were all references to the arts, musical education, physical education, religious education, sex education, science or a second language. Although teachers accepted that aims in these areas were valid for the primary school most were congregated towards the bottom of the list indicating their relatively lower importance. As teachers were free to allocate as many high ratings as they wished (all seventy-two aims *could* have been rated as of the utmost importance) there is clear evidence of discrimination in these areas. The skills of communicating through writing also appear in the lower half of the order as do aims concerning the development of intellectual autonomy. For example, forming a considered opinion and being critical and discriminating were rated in fiftieth and tied fifty-seventh position respectively!

Having looked at the opinions of teachers as a whole the investigators then went on to explore whether there was a wide consensus of opinion among different kinds of teachers (teachers had given information about themselves in the first section of the questionnaire). By and large very few differences emerged. However, teachers who were older, more experienced and more established strongly preferred the societal view of education with its concern to equip the child, personally and practically, to fit into society. They considered moral and spiritual/religious development the two most important aspects and they much preferred traditional and very traditional teaching roles and emphasised those aims which related to the personal, social/moral and spiritual/religious areas. Teachers who were younger, less experienced and less established still tended to give more weight to the societally oriented purpose of education but they gave much more emphasis to the individually oriented view than their older colleagues. Emotional/personal development was seen as a most important aspect and there was a very strong preference for a progressive teaching role. In the intellectual arena the longer-established teachers strongly favoured the basic skills whereas their less established and less experienced colleagues favoured intellectual autonomy.

As the investigators emphasise, the purpose of the project was not to be prescriptive but to examine and open up the question of what primary teachers think. However, in reflecting on the implications of their results they suggest that any rethinking about the aims of primary education might start from the apparent tendency for the individualistic and societal views of education to be in conflict. Although different educationalists have stressed one approach more than the other at different times, and teachers are likely to have come across support for both approaches, there are good reasons for consider-ing both as valid (Dearden in Peters, 1969) and attempting a synthesis between them (Hirst and Peters, 1970).

The investigators followed up their national survey with a number of exploratory studies focusing on more specific questions. One was con-cerned with the extent to which teachers of different age groups (five-year-olds, seven-year-olds, nine-year-olds and eleven-year-olds) saw themselves as contributing to each of the seventy-two aims in their *own* teaching (teachers in the national survey had been asked to think of children at the *end* of their primary education) (Taylor and Holley, 1975). The study showed that teachers of different age groups shared a broad common outlook although teachers of older children tended to see themselves as contri-buting more, on average, to more of the seventy-two listed aims than those with younger pupils. More-over the emphasis on intellectual development went up as the children's age increased whereas the high priority given to aesthetic-creative aims with the five- and seven-year-olds dropped off by the time the children were nine and eleven.

In a second study a slightly modified version of the original questionnaire was completed by 459 teachers in thirty-five middle and secondary schools who were actively involved with eleven- and twelve-year-olds (Ashton, Kneen, Davies and Holley, 1975). As compared to the national balance of teachers the sample tended to be over-representative of women and under-representative of older teachers and teachers in secondary modern schools. Nevertheless there was a high match with the opinions of the national sample of primary teachers although secondary teachers gave slightly greater emphasis to the basic skills whereas the primary teachers gave slightly greater emphasis to skills which enabled children to function adequately in their daily lives.

In a third study 348 tutors in fourteen colleges, all concerned with teaching primary students, completed the questionnaire (Ashton, Kneen, Davies and Holley, 1975). There was wide general agreement with the teachers. Where differences occurred they were consistently in the direction of tutors being more progressive and child-centred and the teachers being more traditional and teacher-directed. However, there was one interesting exception to the overall consensus, perhaps explainable in terms of teachers' direct involvement with children. The teachers were more concerned with children's personal development, particularly with respect to behaviour, whereas in general the tutors were appreciably more interested in children's

higher-level intellectual development. As the investigators point out there are practical implications
should these findings be substantiated by further
evidence. For instance, better feedback is needed
from teachers of two or three years' standing to the
colleges about the shifts of emphasis they had found
necessary once they had started teaching. In addition
in-service work on higher-order intellectual aims
seems desirable once teachers feel established.

In attempting to chart views about the aims of
primary education this chapter has ranged over a
fairly wide area and looked at the findings of a somewhat assorted group of investigations. These have
included the open-ended enquiries of the Plowden
Report, an in-depth study of a single American
experimental programme modelled on informal
British practices, an analysis of some of the writings
of famous educators and an account of the largest
survey of teacher opinion on aims ever undertaken
in this country. A number of interrelated issues have
been pinpointed. For instance, how can the societal
and individualistic views of society be synthesised?
What would this synthesis mean in terms of the
emphasis given to various aspects of development
and to different aims? What would be the implications for the teacher's role, both in general
strategy and in terms of the specific types of activities
in which she should engage?

At this point it is perhaps opportune to ask where
all this leaves the teacher who wishes to review or
reappraise her aims. Where can she turn for
guidance? For a thorough insight into the
fundamental issues raised in this chapter there is no
substitute for returning to the original sources and

taking a close look at what leading philosophers and educational writers have had to say. However, when the teacher comes to evaluate her own practices, and translate her ideas into action, the guidelines mapped out in a book which stemmed from the Aims of Primary Education project described above may well prove useful. It is called *Aims into Practice in the Primary School* (Ashton, Kneen and Davies, 1975) and its advice is based on strategies tried out by teachers. For help in deciding how well policies are working with individual children the *Match and Mismatch* publications can be recommended (Harlen, Darwin and Murphy, 1977). They are concerned with helping teachers match children's learning experiences to development in the various skills, concepts and attitudes involved. Once again the guidelines are firmly rooted in classroom experience and reflect the efforts of teachers to work out ways of diagnosing children's learning by observing them at work. The emphasis is on progress in learning science but much of what is written is equally relevant to other areas of the curriculum as well. Finally, of course, the teacher can look at what educational research has discovered about the implications of different practices. That is the purpose of the following chapters.

It must not be forgotten that the business of translating aims into practice does not take place in a vacuum — the teacher may have to contend with all kinds of pressures which affect what she does or make it impossible for her to operate in ways which she would ideally choose. Although it is convenient to think separately of aims and practice as two distinct entities the distinction is rather artificial. As emphasised earlier in this chapter the two are very closely linked. What the teacher does may be influenced by her ideological stance but equally what she tries to aim for may very well be tempered by a realistic appraisal of what she has found feasible in practice: aims are not just determined by historical influences or personal philosophical standpoints but are open to the influences of others. No doubt teachers who are interested in the conditions affecting the wider framework of their jobs could make a shrewd guess as to what some of these influences might be. This indeed was the starting point of a small and fascinating investigation which focused on teachers' perceptions of the physical, ideological and personal constraints and influences which affected what was taught in primary schools (Taylor, Reid, Holley and Exon, 1974). This chapter will close with a brief look at the study and its principal findings.

One hundred and twenty teachers in twelve primary schools in an urban area in one L.E.A. completed a specially devised questionnaire. The schools were chosen as 'typical' by the local advisers. The questionnaire collected personal information about the teachers and also probed their attitudes to stating aims, to teaching roles (child-centred or teacher-centred) and to curricular change and innovation. It was mainly concerned, however, with the aims of primary education and the influences and constraints on what happens in practice. Eight purposes of primary education were listed and teachers were asked to decide which two they would emphasise most and which two they would emphasise least. They were also asked to consider twenty-eight persons and organisations (local and national, professional and lay) and rate how much each one influenced their school in general and their classroom in particular using a five-point scale (a very strong influence, a strong influence, a definite influence, only of little influence, of no influence at all). They also indicated whether they felt able to reciprocate the influence by making their views known 'if only indirectly'. Finally they put a cross against any of twenty-five listed factors which they felt made for real difficulties in achieving the aims of their teaching or the aims of their school.

The teachers generally were by no means agreed about the emphasis to be placed on different aims. No single aim stood out as outstandingly important although those relating to intellectual capabilities, social awareness and physical and emotional development were generally considered of comparably high importance. Preparation for secondary education, practical skills, moral awareness and aesthetic awareness came next. Spiritual development received least emphasis. Interestingly enough few differences emerged between different groups of teachers except that junior teachers emphasised spiritual development, intellectual capabilities, preparation for secondary education, moral awareness and social awareness more often than infant teachers. They, in turn, emphasised aesthetic awareness, practical skills and physical and emotional development more than junior teachers. Within each school the level of consensus tended to be low or non-existent. The analysis of the perceived influences on what actually happens at school and in the classroom showed that the school and the classroom were seen as two separate zones. The teacher saw herself as having considerable influence in the classroom though not so much within the school where the head was seen as having greatest influence. Whereas the system of influences on what was taught in the classroom was almost entirely grounded in the professional and personal autonomy of the teacher the influences on the school curriculum had a broader base and focused 'upon the interests of children and, to a lesser extent, their parents, on the views of teachers and other educationists about what to teach them, and on the technical, pedagogic, physical and administrative support provided by a variety of agencies' (Taylor, Reid, Holley and Exon, 1974). There was wide variation in the extent to which teachers felt that each influence could be reciprocated and a low general level of perceived reciprocity. Nevertheless teachers' ratings of constraints suggested that in general they did not see themselves as operating in a severely constraining environment. The more commonly experienced ones were the number of children in the class, the size and design of class-rooms, the storage space available, the provision of materials and ancillary help, liaison between schools and the children's home environment. The analysis of teachers' attitudes revealed that on the whole teachers inclined to child-centredness. Much more important, however, was the finding that teachers did not see much merit in stating aims with precision nor in fundamentally reappraising them.

Given the magnitude and complexity of the issues at stake it is perhaps hardly surprising that teachers seemed to baulk at the notion of reflecting on aims. However, it has been the main argument of this whole chapter that teachers should respond to the challenge of thinking, in depth, about what they are trying to do. They regard themselves, in the class-room at least, as being the major influence on what happens and few report severe constraints. Their sense of professional and personal autonomy looms large. Given these perceptions, the pluralist and changing nature of society, the long tradition of professional freedom and the wealth of practical experience which abounds, the teacher (and her children) has much to gain and little to lose by critical reflection and discussion of what she is trying to do. In the long term her professional development may rest on it.

3

Classroom Organisation

Most teachers would probably agree that good classroom organisation is an essential ingredient of
successful teaching. Some might go even further and
suggest that it holds the key. Be that as it may, there
are few more immediate practical considerations
facing the teacher as she starts each new school year
than deciding how to lay out her classroom, group
her children and arrange how they are to spend their
time. And once the term is under way the teacher
will still probably make a whole host of organisational choices as she adjusts her framework to
meet a constant flow of changing needs. Should she
set aside a 'quiet' corner? Abandon her desk to
improve circulation round the room? Introduce a
period for individual topic work? Increase the time
set aside for reading?

Against this background it is perhaps rather
surprising that until recently the topic of classroom
organisation attracted very little interest amongst researchers. Indeed, even now it would be true to say
that not much is known about how teachers
organise their classrooms, their children and their
time and even less is known about the effectiveness

of different ploys although a start (albeit a controversial one) has been made in this direction (Bennett, 1976). This dearth of information can hardly be explained in terms of a general lack of interest in organisational matters. Until recently, streaming, for instance, was the subject of heated debate and prompted one of the largest researches ever conducted in primary education in this country (Barker Lunn, 1970). Nor can it be explained by the rarity of teacher involvement in organisational concerns. A detailed breakdown of how primary teachers spent their day showed that only about half their 'teaching' time was spent on teaching! About a quarter was taken up by control and supervision, clerical and mechanical tasks and pastoral care, and almost all the remainder was spent on matters like grouping children, handing out assignments, arranging the collection or distribution of books and equipment and so forth (Hilsum and Cane, 1971). It seems likely that a major reason for our ignorance about current methods of classroom organisation stems from the fact that the swing away from more traditional strategies has tended to be both initiated and implemented at classroom level. This has meant that no-one is very clear about the overall picture for the country as a whole and that many interesting and original ideas stemming from localised initiatives never reach the wider audience they deserve. The absence of reliable up-to-date information has enabled inaccurate notions to get well entrenched about what is really happening inside the schools. The confusion is exacerbated by reports given by visitors who have been ushered into show schools and the impressions gained by parents when they collect their children at four o'clock. They look into the classroom and see very little which reminds them of their own schooldays.

The purpose of this chapter is to bring together what is known about the ways in which teachers organise their classroom with a view to mapping out some of the alternatives which exist and exposing some of the myths which abound, perhaps more commonly in other countries than here. Interestingly enough, the feeling that something was amiss with the common image of British primary school classrooms, as places virtually free of conflict and coercion, prompted a fascinating American case study in Leicester and Leicestershire schools. It analysed classroom life in terms of how teachers resolved various dilemmas. For instance, should they set or maintain standards for children's learning and development or let children set their own (Berlak, *et al.*, 1975)? The latter part of the chapter examines the effectiveness of different organisational strategies, an issue brought into controversial and sharp relief by the publication of an exploratory study which looked specifically at the relationship between different styles and children's academic progress (Bennett, 1976). A good starting place in any discussion of classroom organisation is, however, to take a close look at what is meant by those well-known catch-terms, 'family grouping' and the 'integrated day'.

Family grouping and the integrated day are probably the two most famous organisational ploys associated with the new developments in primary education. Both strategies share the distinction of exposure to a wider audience by means of books written by teachers with practical knowledge of the innovations they write about. Family (or vertical) grouping is the policy of letting children stay in the same class with the same teacher for several years. Each year the oldest children move up leaving room for some new entrants. Ridgway and Lawton (1968) give a first-class account of what is involved in their well-known book, *Family Grouping in the Primary School.* Unfortunately research evidence on the merits and drawbacks of vertical grouping is lacking. However, its advocates claim that the classroom atmosphere is more relaxed because the older children are well settled and help the younger members. This in turn helps the teacher. They also argue that variations and fluctuations in children's development and interests can be accommodated readily. Furthermore when all the children from one family pass through the same class there is a golden opportunity for establishing good home links. The critics of family grouping argue that excessive demands are made on the teacher because she is switching style constantly to deal with children at very different developmental levels. There is also the suspicion that older children may be insufficiently stretched and the worry that if a child and teacher do not hit it off they may have to live together for a long time. Given all these considerations, how popular has family grouping become? In one study of the organisational policies adopted by junior teachers in two L.E.A.s only a quarter had children of mixed ages and only the same proportion kept their children for two or more years. Both patterns were found almost exclusively in small and medium-sized schools. This rather suggests that vertical grouping can reflect practical necessity as well as pedagogical theory. A village school, for instance, might have two teachers to cope with sixty seven- to eleven-year-olds (Bealing, 1972). This is a good illustration of how a policy born out of administrative necessity can reappear in a different guise with a new lease of life. Open-plan schools are another: witness the one-room village schools of an earlier generation.

No account of life in a modern primary school classroom would be complete without reference to that other fashionable and well-worked concept, the integrated day. Yet the term received not one mention in the Plowden Report (1967) although the notion of an integrated curriculum was expounded:

> children's learning does not fit into subject categories. The younger the children, the more undifferentiated their curriculum will be. As children come towards the top of the junior school ... the conventional subjects become more relevant; some children can then profit from a direct approach to the structure of a subject. Even so, subjects merge and overlap and it is easy for this to happen when one teacher is in charge of the class for most of the time. Schools and individual teachers group subjects in various ways, as well as allowing for work which cuts right across them. (para. 555)

The authors of the Plowden Report put forward a number of practices which expressed this concept of a flexible and integrated curriculum, strategies like project and topic work and taking children out into their local environment. Clearly this concept of the

curriculum could have far-reaching implications
for classroom organisation, yet organisation, as
such, received but scant mention in the Report and
then only in the context of the consequences of an
integrated curriculum on the timetable. However,
the application of the word 'integrated' soon spread
beyond Plowden's original usage and 1968 saw the
publication of that famous and much-quoted book
by Brown and Precious, *The Integrated Day in the
Primary School.*

The term 'integrated day', with its multiplicity of
connotations, implicit values, untested assumptions and wide-ranging implications for the curriculum, classroom organisation and teaching
methods, was almost bound to become highly
emotive. One colourful analogy likened it to the
concept of a permissive society (Dearden 1971):

> Each is felt to be amongst us and to be
> increasingly prevalent. Each tends to arouse
> passions and to cause people to take sides. And in
> the case of neither is there an authoritative
> original doctrine which can be pointed to, and to
> which anyone irritated by vagueness might go
> with relief for an account of the 'real meaning' of
> the term. (page 45)

Integration, according to the Concise Oxford
Dictionary, refers to the combining of parts into a
whole. As a first step to clarifying what the integrated day might mean it is useful to consider which
aspects of education *can* be integrated or combined
(which is not at all the same thing as saying which
parts *should* be so treated). The philosopher Dearden
argued that the concept of the integrated day must be

linked to actual practice and that it was applicable
to talk of an integrated curriculum (like the authors
of the Plowden Report) and integrated organisation
(Dearden, 1971). He suggested that the so-called
minimum concept of the integrated day was:

> a school day so organized that there are no, or at
> least very few, uniform and formalized breaks in
> the activities of learning and teaching, but rather
> a variety of such activities going on simul-
> taneously and changing very much at the choice
> of the individual child, or perhaps of the
> group. (page 47)

Dearden believed that many ideas on aims, curriculum and method were compatible with this
minimum concept defined in essentially organisational language. How compatible is this definition
with what teachers mean when they use the term?

One investigator followed up this question by
conducting a survey of 181 infant and junior
teachers who claimed that they used some form of
integrated day and had attended a weekend con-
ference at Exeter University on the topic (Moran,
1971). He used a questionnaire to pose eight open-
ended questions about classroom practices and
working on the basis of teachers' reports concluded
that the term 'integrated day' was used to refer to
widely different types of organisation in which
children were engaged in several ongoing activities
within the classroom. The degree of choice of
activity for the child varied according to the type of
organisation employed. Many teachers did not
allow children a choice of activities in the three Rs
and in not a single classroom did the degree of

children's choice lead to a completely unbroken day. Judging from this survey a variety of ongoing activities appears to be one essential attribute of what teachers choose to call the integrated day. How widespread is this particular practice?

A small exploratory survey in two L.E.A.s looked at how 189 junior teachers organised their classrooms, regardless of whether they believed they operated any form of integrated day (Bealing, 1972). Virtually every teacher reported that activities in several curricular areas took place simultaneously for at least part of the time. However, it seems that a myth has grown up about the impact of the so-called primary revolution. The overwhelming majority of children were in unstreamed classes and approximately half the teachers taught under conditions which are often thought to be conducive to experimentation, namely a well-planned and well-established system of comprehensive education and no eleven-plus of any kind. Nevertheless the evidence showed that the integrated day in terms of Dearden's minimum concept (a variety of activities changing very much at children's choice) was a very far cry from reality for most of the teachers.

The study confirmed that the majority of teachers adopted informal group lay-outs for their classrooms although only a small proportion were equipped with modern purpose-built tables or table units. The two most popular plans by far were to sit children in medium-sized groups of five to eight or to have a mixture of medium groups and smaller ones containing up to four children. Most teachers had moved their desk away from the traditional centre position in front of the class. A third reported that they spent most of the time circulating and almost all the remainder said they split their time about equally between circulating and getting children to come to see them at their desk. Many children had the opportunity to work independently outside the classroom on their own or in small groups. There was, however, tight teacher control over where children sat and worked.

Most children know precisely where to sit if the teacher asks them to go to their 'own' places. With only a few exceptions teachers allocated at least some of their class to their 'own' seats or moved children for work in at least one curricular area or did both these things. Within this tight overall structure there was scope for children to move freely without asking permission. For instance, almost all the teachers let children make temporary moves and of these at least 90 per cent thought consulting the teacher, consulting books or collecting books and materials constituted legitimate reasons. However, only a minority allowed children to change their work place without permission.

So much for movement and seating arrangements. Perhaps more surprising than this high measure of teacher control was the finding that almost two-thirds of the teachers who ever directed children to places found occasion to set up a streaming situation in miniature within their classrooms, grouping pupils according to their abilities and attainments. Only about a third ever used mixed ability groups and all-in-all four-fifths of the teachers who directed children made judgements of children's abilities which they used for either homogeneous or heterogeneous ability groupings.

When teachers indicated which factors helped them in their evaluations most used subjective estimates of the children's work standards (80 per cent) and/or reading age (55 per cent). Little heed was paid to I.Q. scores, school tests, standardised attainment tests or the previous teacher's report. This latter finding lends credence to the observation made in Chapter 2 that teachers see themselves as autonomous in their own classrooms.

Teaching methods varied according to the area of the curriculum but, overall, individual work predominated. This was particularly marked for reading where a quarter of the teachers relied totally on this technique. Although few teachers relied solely on group work in any area of the curriculum the majority included it in their repertoire and it gained considerable favour in art and craft, general studies and mathematics. Individual and group work were more popular than classwork but it would be wrong to surmise that class teaching had disappeared. It was much in evidence for all subjects except reading although the proportion of teachers relying solely on this method was extremely low except, strangely, for science where it reached 12 per cent.

Taken together these results put a question mark beside the influence of new ideas. There was so much direct teacher control over matters like where children sat and worked that it seems highly doubtful whether there is much opportunity for children to choose and organise their own activities. A census of the teaching patterns of all third- and fourth-year primary teachers in Lancashire and Cumbria came to a similar conclusion (Bennett, 1976). Teacher control of physical movement and talk was generally high, one-third used some form of internal streaming device and although half the time was spent on individual work, with group work coming next in popularity, teachers reported talking to the whole class for almost one-fifth of the time. Moreover for more than three-quarters of the time children worked on tasks set by the teacher and a subject-centred curriculum seemed to predominate: rather less than a fifth of each week was spent on integrated subjects like environmental studies, project and topic work and free choice periods. Tests were much in evidence and, although very few teachers reported discipline problems and the overwhelming majority found that verbal reproof was normally sufficient, over half admitted to smacking for persistent disruptive behaviour. More detailed analysis found that less than one teacher in ten corresponded closely to the Plowden model.

Although neither of these two investigations are based on a large national representative sample they strongly suggest that a myth has grown up about the impact of the so-called primary revolution. This is not to say that there have been no impressive changes and developments, indeed many areas of Britain can boast a number of outstanding innovative schools. However, taking the country as a whole the widely propagated image of British classrooms as places where children move about freely, following their own interests and learning through discovery and informal cooperation with each other and the teacher, appears to have been grossly exaggerated. It seems highly improbable that many children have experienced Plowden-inspired teaching.

Given this situation it seems rather unrealistic for

critics of the new ideas to point an accusing finger at the effects of progressive education when they try to understand the shortcomings of our school system. Informal Plowden-style classrooms are too scarce to be responsible for the widespread inadequacies of educational standards which some commentators claim typify the country as a whole. Nevertheless this is not to argue that informal classrooms can or should be immune to comparative appraisals.

It is almost inevitable that any novel or different style of organisation should invite comparison with well-established and well-tried alternatives. All the same it is important to emphasise that the scope for *comparative* evaluations of different organisational approaches is severely limited and circumscribed. Most teachers, whatever their pedagogical persuasion, are concerned with children's proficiency in the basic skills (although they are by no means unanimous in the importance they attach, see Chapter 2). It is therefore wise to monitor and compare children's progress in the three Rs under different regimes. However, very few teachers who adopt, for instance, a very informal style of classroom organisation would rest their case on the supposed superiority of their methods for basic numeracy and literacy. Their choice of approach often reflects a commitment to a far wider range of objectives and aspirations. Organisation cannot be divorced from the teacher's aims, her style of classroom behaviour or her views on the curriculum. Almost every organisational decision can say something about the teacher's philosophy or carry ramifications for what is taught or how it is done. No evaluation of organisational strategies or tactics should neglect this wider context: comparative studies of the efficiency of different approaches are only useful in so far as the different approaches are striving towards the same things. However, this does not mean that the new developments in classroom organisation cannot (or should not) be evaluated.

At least as important as comparative assessment is the job of evaluating whether the claims made for any style are justified (irrespective of whether they are valued by the advocates of alternative approaches) and whether any undesirable by-products exist (irrespective of whether they are known to the teachers who practise the method). Critical discussion is another essential component of evaluation. Any collected information about children, teachers and schools should only supplement rational debate about the fundamental issues underlying different approaches. It should not be used as a substitute. The educational researcher can show that one method is superior or comparable to another on certain criteria, he can examine some of the claims and document some of the consequences, desired or otherwise, of different approaches. However, he cannot prove in any absolute sense of the word that one style of classroom organisation is better than another. It is totally impossible to demonstrate in scientific terms that a deep musical appreciation is preferable to a well-developed artistic talent, that honesty is preferable to kindness or that intellectual autonomy is preferable to intellectual integrity.

The importance of understanding the issues involved in evaluating classroom organisation cannot be overemphasised in the light of what

happened when an exploratory study of the relationship between teaching style (conceived in largely
organisational terms) and pupil progress (measured
by conventional paper and pencil tests) hit the head-
lines (Bennett, 1976). The findings were widely
represented as a wholesale indictment of modern
ideas and practice and *The Times* ran a leader
entitled 'Progress is not progressive' (26 April 1976).
The fact that one relatively small investigation
should stir up such a hornets' nest is indicative of
widespread professional and public concern with
modern methods (the report was published in the
aftermath of the William Tyndale affair). It also
highlights the dearth of high quality information
referred to earlier in this chapter and the general lack
of understanding about what a comprehensive
evaluation entails. In the light of all the controversy
it is only too easy to forget what the study really did
and what it actually showed.

At the start of his enquiries Bennett distributed a
questionnaire to all the third- and fourth-year
junior teachers working in Lancashire's and
Cumbria's 871 primary schools. The questionnaire
was divided into three sections. The first part
requested personal details about the teacher and
information about her class and classroom, the
second was concerned with her teaching methods
(under the sub-headings seating arrangements, classroom organisation, organising the curriculum,
testing and marking, discipline and allocation of
teaching time) and the third part sought her
opinions on various aims, education issues and
teaching methods. Some of the findings of this
survey have already been mentioned earlier in this

chapter and in Chapter 2, but the really controversial results stemmed from the second phase of the investigation. The 468 fourth-year teachers were grouped into twelve categories on the basis of their reported teaching approach using a statistical technique called cluster analysis. Checks were then made to ensure that these twelve groups were a true reflection of classroom differences. Research staff and L.E.A. advisers visited thirty-seven of the teachers and their children wrote an essay entitled 'What I did at school yesterday'. Neither the research staff nor the advisers nor, of course, the children knew the group in which the teacher had been placed. However, their reports corresponded closely to the descriptions of the groups in which the teachers had been placed by the cluster analysis. This suggested that the classification system had a sound basis.

The thirty-seven teachers who were visited came from seven of the twelve categories (clusters). These seven were chosen because they represented the whole range and could be collapsed conveniently into three general styles — informal, formal and mixed. The particular teachers were picked because their teaching profiles most closely matched the central profiles of the clusters from which they came. Initially twelve teachers were selected to represent each of the three general styles but one of the informal classes was small and so an additional informal teacher was included. Taken together these staff were responsible for about 1,200 children, of whom approximately 400 were taught by informal methods, 400 by mixed methods and 400 by formal methods.

All 1,200 children did a number of tests. At the end of their third year, and again at the end of their fourth year, the children were tested in reading, mathematics and English. This enabled their progress over the year to be assessed. In the Autumn term the children also wrote an imaginative story on the topic of 'Invisibility' and a descriptive account (already referred to) on what they had done at school the previous day. In addition, at the start and finish of their fourth year, they also completed a large battery of personality tests. Apart from these test data on children's academic progress and personality, a number of children were observed during normal class activities using a specially designed record sheet. All in all 101 children drawn from both formal and informal classrooms were observed.

The study came up with a number of well-publicised findings. Pupils taught by formal styles showed superior progress in reading, mathematics and English to those taught by informal styles and also (with the exception of reading) to those taught with mixed methods. The children who still took the eleven-plus also showed superior progress, especially in reading. Formal pupils were better at punctuation, the same in spelling and no worse in imaginative story writing.

The progress made by different types of children experiencing different teaching styles was also examined. The children were grouped into eight categories by means of a cluster analysis of the information they had supplied about themselves on the personality tests. Some interesting results emerged. It was found, for instance, that the so-called 'saints', who were stable, extroverted, motivated and conforming, substantially over-achieved with formal teaching and under-achieved with informal methods. This pattern was repeated with some of the other types of children as well. Mixed teaching was particularly unsuccessful for pupils who were un-motivated and introverted although marginally most productive with the so-called 'sinners', the children who were both contentious and non-conforming. However, despite the fact that children's personalities affected their attainment, the most interesting finding was that the influence of their teachers' styles was much greater. This was also the case with the behavioural demands of the different teaching styles to which children were exposed. When children were observed in their class-rooms it was found that these demands tended to obliterate the influence of their personalities on how they behaved. Nevertheless some differences between different types of children did emerge. For instance in informal classrooms children who were neurotic or contentious spent considerably less time on work-related activities than their less neurotic and non-contentious peers. Their work levels were comparable in formal classrooms.

On the face of it these findings provide a rather dismal commentary on the deficiencies of informal teaching: they were certainly heralded as such by those who would like to see a retrenchment in tradi-tional methods. Without doubt they relate to two important issues, namely children's proficiency in the basic skills and the abilities of different types of children to profit from different kinds of teaching. It is part of the conventional wisdom, to say nothing of

Plowden, that different kinds of children require different kinds of handling and yet here is some evidence which presents a *prima facie* case that on the whole formal methods are best for most pupils. It therefore becomes extremely important to scrutinise the quality of the evidence. It is here that the limitations of the study show: it is an interesting and timely piece of exploratory research looking at issues of widespread public disquiet. However, the study is by no means definitive. Its conclusions are based on just thirty-seven fourth-year junior classrooms and critics have raised a whole host of questions. How representative are these teachers of primary teachers as a whole? The formal teachers were more experienced — did this affect the results? Socio-economic class is the most accurate predictor of attainment available and yet no information is provided about the children's home background — was it comparable in the formal and informal classrooms? Children's familiarity with different teaching methods as they come up through the primary school may well influence their progress under different regimes — were the children in formal and informal classrooms thoroughly accustomed to these different styles?.

Leaving aside issues of this type, together with various technical doubts and arguments about the teacher sample and the statistical interpretation of the results (Gray and Satterly, 1976; Bennett and Entwistle, 1977), the study's most important limitation centres around the task of assessment itself. All the tests were of the pencil and paper variety. Children in formal classrooms were much more likely to be practised at taking tests of this kind and much more motivated to perform well, particularly as many still sat the eleven-plus. Indeed half the teachers who took part in the study felt that the tests favoured formal teaching (although a third thought there was no bias and a sixth considered the tests favoured informal teaching). This thorny question of what makes a 'fair' test relates to the wider issue of what you choose to measure, that is to say, to the criteria you think important. Whilst many people would be willing to accept the validity of the tests used to measure progress in the basic skills (given certain reservations) few are happy with the tests of creative and descriptive writing. Not only were they one-off checks (thus debarring any assessment of progress) but their scope was so limited (a single piece of work in each case) that they provide little or no basis for generalisation, let alone comparison. Moreover large areas of children's learning were left totally unexplored, for instance high-level cognitive concepts, affective development and social skills. This is not a criticism of the research itself — no one study can cover everything — but it is a criticism of those who use the results to argue, without more ado, for a renewed emphasis on the old proven methods of teaching. Such arguments reveal little understanding of the nature of evaluation (and the fact that no amount of social scientific enquiry can prove the absolute superiority of one approach over another) and an incredibly narrow outlook on education where basic skills, even if it means rote learning and 'barking at words', are prized to the exclusion of everything else. A look back at the Aims of Primary Education project discussed in Chapter 2 confirms that teachers at least, whatever their pedagogical perspective, do not hold this view.

What lessons can the teacher learn from this

research? How relevant is it to her own decisions and ideas on classroom organisation? In practical terms it offers little guidance and it certainly should not make her feel guilty or defensive if she prefers informal methods. As already explained, a choice of organisational strategies requires critical reflection as well as researcher's 'facts' and this is particularly so when the 'facts' in question are neither wide-ranging nor well-established. However, the findings relate to significant issues and should alert the teacher to possible strengths and weaknesses in her own theory and practice, to assets and limitations of which she may be only partially aware. Is she giving the right amount of time and energy to the basic skills? Can she justify her policies in these areas to herself in intellectually acceptable terms? Can she explain her rationale to people who may have a legitimate concern in her class's progress, to parents, employers and so on? Are her other aspirations for children's progress in the fields of expressive and creative activities, scientific enquiries and so forth being realised? Are any individuals or groups of children suffering under her particular regime? Is she happy with the 'quality' of life, with what is happening right now, in her classroom?

As a final comment on this weighty topic of class-room organisation, it is worthwhile pointing out that one classroom in the Bennett study was categorised as high gain in every achievement area and in one particular area came out top of all the thirty-seven classrooms investigated. The content of the curriculum was clearly organised and well structured and a lot of time was spent on English and mathematics. The teacher was informal in style.

This raises the feasible notion that a structured and cognitively-oriented curriculum may be one way to success in the basic skills in the informal classroom. In any event it gives a much needed boost to the argument that 'informal' is not necessarily synonymous with 'mess 'n' muddle'. The path ahead is surely for informal educators to impress upon the public as a whole the variety of structure and organisation which exists in informal classrooms and at the same time to concentrate on how these might be further developed. One thing is sure, there is nothing more fruitless (and potentially more harmful) than a rigid, polarised animosity between the proponents of formal and informal methods. As this chapter has shown the situation at classroom level cannot be neatly dichotomised into 'chalk and talk' and 'discovery learning' (or any of the other pairs of labels which abound). It is far more complex than that. Moreover the questions at issue do not lend themselves to black or white answers. They are far more involved than is often supposed. It is clear that for good or for ill the preoccupation with standards is with us. Would it be going too far to suggest that teachers have an obligation to widen the basis of this debate?

4

Individual Attention

'. . . any class, however homogeneous it seems, must always be treated as a body of children needing individual and different attention' (para. 75). Thus runs one of the Plowden Report's most well-known recommendations. It is based on the argument that there are great individual differences between children, even between those of the same age, and it reflects the authors' deep conviction that it is the child who 'lies at the heart of the educational process' (para. 9). This sentiment finds a very prominent expression in the title emblazoned on the Report's cover, *Children and their Primary Schools (1967)*.

The notion of individual attention is central to modern thinking. It has been emphasised time and time again in the literature (see Chapter 2) and the related concept of individual work has found a prominent place in the repertoire of many teachers (see Chapter 3). Although these two techniques of individual attention and individual work may go hand in hand it is important to differentiate between them. Individual attention occurs when the teacher interacts privately with a single child. By contrast individual work takes place when all the children have different tasks, frequently drawn from a wide range of curricular areas. When individual work is in progress the teacher is almost bound to favour individual attention as well because no two children are doing the same thing. However, the converse is not true. It is quite possible for all the class to have identical work and for the teacher to still prefer talking privately to individual children. Indeed this is an oft-used ploy of some otherwise very traditional teachers. Private individual attention, and its merits and drawbacks, is therefore not an exclusive feature of informal teaching and consequently warrants the consideration of a wide audience.

Few teachers would dispute the desirability of individual attention under ideal circumstances, although some remain sceptical of its feasibility in normal conditions. Moreover opinions vary as to when it is most appropriate and how it should be implemented. Some teachers rely on individual attention almost entirely, others mix it up with group or class teaching; some use it more with their most able children, some with their least; some favour it more in some curricular areas, some in others; some circulate around the class talking to the children who seek them out or to those they think need help, others sit at their desk and get the children to queue. The permutations on the uses of individual attention are endless and it is probably true to say that most teachers, if not all, spend at least part of their time dealing privately with children one at a time.

Such a system makes heavy demands on the teacher even if all the children have similar work in the same area of the curriculum. One investigator working in an infant school in a working-class area of south-east London estimated that the four teachers she watched averaged one hundred and twenty contacts with children an hour, of which the overwhelming majority were brief, consisting of no more than four teacher comments or questions (Resnick, 1972). Another researcher working in an infant school in north-west London found an even higher rate. When he tallied the teacher's interactions for two ten-minute periods in each of four classrooms he found approximately three per minute during independent activity periods. During group discussions when teachers were eliciting news, reactions and experiences from children the rate was usually even greater (Brandt, 1975). All these findings illustrate that a system based on individual attention adds up to an extremely industrious and taxing rate of switching attention for the teacher. It is therefore easy to forget that in terms of individual contact, children in a class of forty could only expect to see the teacher on their own for ninety seconds in each hour *if* they received an equal share of time, and this is a big if.

Carefully documented records have confirmed what most teachers would suspect, namely that the distribution of the teacher's help in terms of the number of contacts with each child is anything but equal (Garner and Bing, 1973). The usual answer is that this does not really matter because the greatest merit of individual attention is that the teacher can arrange the children's activities in such a way that only a manageable proportion of the class requires much in the way of guidance and supervision at any given moment. The teacher uses her professional judgement to decide who to help and who to leave alone at any given point in time. This particular line of reasoning implies that the teacher is suffi-ciently in control of classroom events to be able to implement her desired policy and focus on the children she considers to require the most attention. It also suggests that an equal distribution of teacher contact could be more worrying than an uneven spread. It might mean, for instance, that the teacher was not responding sensitively enough to the indivi-dual differences in personality, attainment and interests amongst the members of her class and the demands of their particular activities. Is this answer satisfactory? Does it go far enough? In brief, the available evidence suggests that the reply to both these questions is no.

A small and simple study with thirteen- and fourteen-year-olds in the U.S.A. would have serious implications for many primary teachers in this country if the same results were found here (Withall, 1956). A teacher's interactions were recorded during informally run art classes. The number of teacher contacts with individual children was remarkably uneven but much more important than this was the fact that the recorded pattern was not what the teacher would have liked to have seen. Some of the class were getting more attention than the teacher deemed necessary and others were getting too little. The teacher then went back and tried to bring his actual teaching behaviour into line with his stated intentions about how he was going to spread his time. And what was found? Although the teacher managed to redistribute his attention appreciably his ideal was not reached: indeed, one girl already judged to be receiving too much attention actually managed to increase her share despite the teacher's efforts to cut it down! This is perhaps an all-too-familiar problem for teachers deeply involved in the complex, interweaving flow of classroom activities. It prompts another key question. Are some types of children better able than others to obtain and sustain the scarce commodity of teacher attention?

A study of teacher-pupil contacts in five first-year junior classrooms, this time in Britain, hints that this could be so (Garner and Bing, 1973). When children were observed in their home classrooms for at least six consecutive days it emerged that two main groups of children tended to receive most attention. These were the active hardworkers who sought the teacher out and the active miscreants who invoked the teacher's displeasure. As the investigators concluded: 'If teacher contact is desired then being average and passive ... is not the way to obtain it'. Of course it may be that the teachers concerned had made deliberate decisions to let the average passive children work on their own. This is plausible but unlikely and it is probably much more reasonable to suggest that their relatively low share of the teacher's attention was more to do with other factors which are very difficult to control. For instance the teacher may find it takes very considerable skill to stave off active children who persistently approach her without undermining their initiative and it may prove just as difficult to ensure that timid children pluck up courage to ask for help. And incidentally it is worth while pointing out that resorting to traditional types of classroom lay-outs and methods of teaching would not necessarily mean that children received more equable shares of the teacher's attention. A small study of teachers in action in more formal classrooms spanning the primary and secondary range in the U.S.A. found that the teacher interacted most with those children seated in a 'V' which was wide at the front and narrowed to a point in the back row (Adams and Biddle, 1970). Once again it is difficult to believe that this was altogether the teachers' deliberate policy.

Given the small amount of individual attention that the average child is likely to receive, and given its almost certain uneven spread amongst different children, it may well be that the quality of the contact when it does occur is of very great importance. One interesting exploratory study carried out in Scotland suggested that this could indeed be so (Cameron-Jones and Reid, 1972). It looked at the progress made in reading comprehension by nineteen backward readers. They were all seven-year-olds and received two kinds of reading instruction each day. They were taught in their own class by their class teacher alongside their classmates and in addition received forty minutes of extra help with a remedial teacher in a small group of no more than eight pupils in a different room in their school. Their progress was compared with nineteen other children of similar reading ability, intelligence, age and social class who attended schools in a similar neighbourhood. The schools had similar physical facilities and their general teaching methods showed a similar degree of progressiveness. Quite predictably the children who received remedial help made greater advances. The study then concentrated on the verbal behaviour of teachers in ordinary and remedial classrooms so that the amount and kind of attention received by pupils in these two situations could be compared. Not unexpectedly it was found that in the remedial setting children were more likely to have conversations on their own with the teacher, be given their own personal assignments to do and have their work assessed on an individual basis. The small size of the remedial classes was clearly conducive to individual attention. However, much more interesting than this was the fact that children in the remedial setting received more comparative comment about their work and progress. Moreover the remedial teachers made more references to the child himself ('Much better than you did before') than the class teachers. In ordinary classrooms the teacher was more likely to compare a pupil with other children ('Now you're right past John') than in the remedial setting. Clearly such a small study cannot prove conclusively that subtle differences of this type in the ongoing process of teaching reading were responsible for the remedial children's greater progress. Other factors like the overall amount of time spent on reading and the overall amount of individual attention may be equally important. Nevertheless the observed differences in how teachers talked to children in the two settings are clearly worthy of further consideration. Audience size and the kinds of conversation used may be very important for learning and not only for the learning of remedial children.

Teachers show a great range of styles for talking to

children, as reflected in their preferences for audiences of different sizes and their emphases on different types of conversational content. What is the effect of different styles on the knowledge, skills and attitudes that children acquire? What is the effect of different styles on different children? Unfortunately there has been very little investigation of these crucial questions although a small exploratory study has thrown some light on the type of conversation which can occur when teachers rely heavily on private individual attention (Boydell, 1974).

Information was collected by six observers (themselves teachers) who were trained to use an observation schedule which had been specifically designed for use in informal junior school classrooms. Every twenty-five seconds a pre-recorded time signal was fed into the observer's ear from a small cassette tape recorder and the observer coded the size of the teacher's audience and the nature of her conversation at the precise time of the signal. The observer did this on a specially prepared record sheet by marking one of three possible audience categories (addressing children as a whole class, talking to a small group or giving private individual attention) and one of nineteen possible conversation categories. Each of these nineteen categories fell into one of six major groups. The groups were based on what the teacher was talking about (task, task supervision or routine matter) and whether or not the teacher was seeking an answer (question or statement).

When fully trained each of the six observers visited each of six volunteer junior teachers in turn.

This rotation of observers meant that every teacher was seen once by every observer. Without exception it was found that all six teachers in this study relied heavily on individual attention, talking privately to children one at a time for at least 70 per cent of the observed lesson time. Indeed one of the teachers averaged almost 90 per cent on this type of contact. The teachers were not asked to lay on a demonstration of individual attention for the purpose of the study: the heavy use was entirely their own choice. The teachers, three men and three women, were in many ways representative of junior teachers as a whole. They worked in six different unstreamed city schools, averaged three years' teaching experience and had an average class size of thirty-one children. Four taught lower juniors and two taught upper juniors. All the children worked at mathematics during each visit and sat informally in small groups, sometimes in groups of similar ability. In some lessons all the children had the same task, in others there was a variety of activities. All in all a very wide range of mathematics work was observed, sometimes even within the same classroom.

The analysis of the teachers' conversation during these mathematics lessons showed that on average they were spending half their time on task supervision ('Have you finished yet?'; 'That answer's not quite right'). The remainder of the time was divided almost equally between the task itself ('How could you work out the answer?'; 'This is called a plumb line') and routine matters ('Please open the window'; 'Stop being silly'). Thus three-quarters of the teachers' entire conversation could be called work-oriented because it was to do with the children's task or its ongoing supervision. Only a quarter fell outside this area with its focus on routine classroom business.

Does this correspond to the child's eye view, to what the child hears the teacher say? The short answer is no. As a result of further analysis it was estimated that although the teacher only spent a quarter of her time on routine matters like classroom organisation and discipline, routine comments figured prominently in the contacts children received. The explanation for this paradox is simple. Children received such little teacher contact of any kind (individual attention, group member, class member) that the few remarks about routine matters which the teacher addressed to the class as a whole formed a large proportion of what they heard the teacher say. Their experience of work-oriented conversation is considerably less than the simple analysis of teacher talk might suggest.

Against this background it seems to be more important than ever to look closely at the nature of the teacher's work-oriented contact. As already mentioned it was largely supervisory. Particularly common were comments telling the child what to do or how to do it and evaluative remarks about his work, although in this context it is interesting to note that praise was rarely recorded. More interesting still, however, was the finding that even when contacts about the substantive content of children's tasks occurred they were often of a low cognitive order, consisting of questions answered by recalling facts and factual teacher statements. High-level cognitive contributions involving ideas, explanations and problems only accounted for about one-tenth of the teacher's total conversation. Moreover, open-ended questions about the children's task activities (where the teacher was prepared to accept a wide range of ideas or solutions) were rarely encountered. One reason for the conversation's relatively low intellectual level might be due to the time pressure caused by the high rate of contact with different children (Garner and Bing, 1973). Another might be teachers' priorities. The Aims of Primary Education Project found that the only major difference of opinion between teachers and tutors was the much greater emphasis that tutors attached to higher-level intellectual aims. Teachers were more concerned with children's personal development, particularly with respect to their behaviour (Ashton, Kneen, Davies and Holley, 1975).

Whatever the underlying causes, the implications of a low intellectual level seem very serious indeed. It is probably not an exaggeration to claim that teacher-pupil contact is a crucial factor in the development of thinking and enquiry skills. And this contact takes on added significance if it occurs in the context of a more 'open' approach to education. 'Open' education has many different nuances and can be defined in many different ways but one definition suggests it implies 'an environment in which the possibility for exploration and learning of self and of the world are unobstructed' (Barth and Rathbone, 1972). As one educator has pointed out, the focus of such open education is 'on learner-based teaching in which there is active involvement of the learner, self-initiated and self-maintained investigation, and several learning

routes "open" from which the learner can choose'
(Tough, 1975). Tough argues that children need
skills of communication and investigation to cope
in open situations. They need, for example, to be
able to report on present and past activities, to see
relationships and give explanations of how and why
certain things happen, to anticipate and plan
activities, to recognise problems and find solutions
to meet them, to predict the consequences of actions
and so forth. It seems likely that these skills are
much more likely to be developed where the child
experiences dialogue in which language is used in
these ways (Tough, 1975):

> If, for example, children are not disposed to
> recognise the relevance of past experience for
> something that is happening in the present, or is
> being anticipated in the near future, then
> dialogue with the teacher (or some other adult
> who is aware of the needs of such children) may be
> the only experience from which children will
> build such awareness. Or again, if children are not
> disposed to look for cause and effect relationships,
> the dialogue in which the child is helped to
> become aware of such relationships becomes a
> necessary experience before he will be oriented to
> look for such relationships for himself. (page 22)

It is, of course, no easy task to talk to children in
such a way that they discover their language
resources and use them to explore the possibilities
inherent in the activity in which they are engaged.
However, without dialogue which clarifies concepts
and values, much of the potential of the concrete
experiences the child meets through devised

activities and materials and school visits may be lost. In addition, even when children can read fluently most need help, through discussion with the teacher, to relate the ideas they have gleaned from books to the tasks they are pursuing (Tough, 1975). Work cards and programmed instruction materials are no substitute for face-to-face encounters between children and teachers. The transcripts in the Rosens' book, *The Language of Primary School Children* (1973), illustrate something of the quality that these encounters can produce, even with so-called disadvantaged children.

Looking at the method of individual attention from the child's point of view several points are very clear. First of all the very limited face-to-face communication with the teacher means that the child rarely hears adult speech, let alone engages in dialogue. Of course this does not mean that his experience of language as a whole is necessarily restricted in the classroom: teachers who rely heavily on individual attention generally permit or encourage children to talk to each other and provision their rooms with an abundance of books, work cards, written materials and programmed instructions of all kinds. None the less these should not be seen as replacements for skilfully handled discussions with the teacher: children left to their own devices may only generate a restricted range of ideas and reading with minimal comprehension is an all-too-familiar problem anyway. And what of the child who is diffident and does not enjoy talking to his neighbours or the poor reader who cannot cope with even the simplest of written materials? For them the classroom could be a place bereft of language, either written or spoken. It is not at all difficult to imagine how language and intellectual development might be greatly impaired under such circumstances. A second problem associated with individual attention is that children have such unequal chances of seeing the teacher that a child might go through an entire lesson without any direct teacher contact. Certain children might be particularly vulnerable to neglect. A child of average ability who is quiet and obedient may be at a decided disadvantage compared to his more active and able classmates and for such a child individual attention may be more akin to no attention. A third problem, possibly deriving from the rate at which the teacher switches her attention, is the low intellectual level of children's contacts with the teacher.

Thus a system rooted in individual attention can have the paradoxical effect that children will find that the teacher leaves them alone for most of the time, spends much more time with some children than others, occasionally singles them out for a few words either on their own (or in small groups) and will periodically talk to them as a class, sometimes about work but almost as often about classroom organisation or behaviour. What a difference to the picture teachers must have with their hundred-plus contacts with children an hour of which the overwhelming majority are individual and work-oriented! Small wonder that some parents pick up strange ideas about modern methods if they probe their offspring's accounts of what they have done at school. Perhaps there is enough evidence to indicate that no matter how distorted these reports sound to the teacher they may have some validity from the child's point of view. Isolation from the teacher, coupled with a fairly high probability that contacts will not be work-oriented, or at any rate not at a very high intellectual level, when they do occur is as much a classroom reality for many children as the exhausting never-ending series of work conversations are for the teacher. Against this background it is easy to forget that 'It's time to pack up', uttered by a weary teacher at the end of the afternoon, could be all some children have heard her say to them all day.

Is the foregoing discussion intended as an indictment of modern methods? The short answer is an unequivocal no. The major aim of this analysis is to highlight some of the problems associated with individual attention and explore some practical solutions.

Consider first the dearth of adult conversation. One obvious way to increase children's exposure to adult speech is through the provision of taped materials of various kinds. This could have clear benefits especially for the poorer readers. Another possibility, already tried out in the Head Start and Follow Through programmes in the U.S.A., is the introduction of aides and parent volunteers working under the teacher's supervision in the classroom. The dangers and drawbacks of such a system are well known and are mostly related to how, in practice, it would be possible to separate teaching from non-teaching jobs during normal lesson time. However, if attention is to be highly individualised it is difficult to see how even the most talented of teachers working alone can deal adequately with the intellectual and socio-emotional needs of thirty-odd children if she is unable to delegate any of the relatively routine but time-consuming jobs like getting out apparatus, mending equipment and taking in dinner money. Smaller classes would clearly improve the situation but it would still remain a moot point as to whether the teacher is best employed on those kinds of activities anyway. In this context it is interesting to note that one of the earliest studies involving classroom observation in Britain was to do with the possibility of employing teaching auxiliaries in Scottish primary schools (Duthie, 1970).

And what of the problem of distributing attention? Each teacher would be well advised to scrutinise her own interaction pattern. If some children are receiving more individual attention than others is her distribution of time in line with some policy? For instance, does it reflect the fact that she is trying to bring every child in the class up to certain minimal standards on the types of growth she prizes, with a consequent bias in favour of those making slower progress? If all is not as she would wish, and certain children are receiving more attention than she thinks warranted, can she gradually influence them to become more self-sufficient? And can she devise techniques for ensuring that no child is inadvertently neglected? One simple and common ploy is for children to place their completed work in a box which can be regularly checked to ensure that no important information about their difficulties and achievements has been overlooked. Another idea, this time for monitoring the amount of teacher contact each pupil receives, is a peg board which lists the children's names one below the other with a separate column and set of coloured pegs for each area of the curriculum. There might be red pegs for reading, blue for creative writing, green for mathematics and so on. At the beginning of the week all the pegs for each child are placed in the first holes in all the columns. Then, for example, each time the teacher hears a child read, she moves the child's red reading peg into the next hole to the right within the reading column. By similarly charting work contacts in all the other areas of the curriculum the teacher can see at a glance who has had a lot of help in mathematics and who has been neglected, say, in environmental studies.

If, despite her best-laid plans, self-monitoring of this kind reveals that the teacher is still not exercising as much control over her interaction pattern as she would wish, it would be wise for her to consider whether any aspects of her classroom environment could be usefully modified. For instance, the physical lay-out of the classroom coupled with ease of movement round the tables may mean that she is spending more time in certain parts of the room than others. Her very proximity may encourage the nearby children to approach her whilst deterring others from making longer or more difficult journeys from across the room.

A final problem associated with the extensive use of individual attention centres on how the cognitive quality of teacher-pupil contact can be raised. The discussion so far has rather implied that there is no viable alternative to a heavy reliance on individual attention. But is this really so? Is there not a case for a more eclectic approach? Given our present state of knowledge and likely staffing resources for the foreseeable future, the wisest course of action may be flexibility in methods of talking to children. Group seating arrangements and group work were found to be extremely common ploys when 189 junior teachers in two L.E.A.s reported on their methods of classroom organisation (Bealing, 1972). These conditions seem extremely conducive to group teaching, yet in practice it seems highly doubtful whether teachers exploit their opportunities for *talking* to groups as much as they could. It is hard to resist the conclusions that three or four children might gain more stimulation at a higher cognitive level from an extended five- or six-minute group discussion with the teacher than from the one or two minutes of private attention they would otherwise receive. This was certainly the opinion expressed in the Plowden Report (para. 755). One or two minutes of individual attention is not always long enough to help a child develop his ideas and motivation sufficiently to enable him to work productively and happily for long periods when the teacher is helping other children. Moreover it allows very little time for the teacher to probe and gather the diagnostic information she requires to assess the child's levels of development, information which is vital if she is to guide the child's learning effectively.

Most teachers from the two L.E.A.s in the survey mentioned above found some use for class work in all areas of the curriculum except reading. Despite the Plowden Report's emphasis on individual attention, it is sometimes forgotten that the authors pointed out the value of class teaching for certain specific purposes like telling a story or giving a vivid reconstruction of the past. They noted that experiences of this type could be heightened by being shared with a class and that they helped to make the class a unity (para. 756). Whilst welcoming the trend towards individual learning the Report recommended a combination of individual, group and class work (para. 833). The available evidence would suggest that many teachers heed this advice although it would be interesting to know how many teachers feel guilty or defensive if they turn aside from individual work and individual attention for very long. One of the problems is that the notions of individual work and attention carry such an air of pedagogic enlightenment and respectability that it is difficult to discuss areas of possible improvement without seeming to undermine the entire viability of the approach. That is certainly not the purpose here: the value of children's uniqueness and the need for the teacher to respond sensitively to their manifold differences are not in dispute. However, there is growing evidence that for some teachers, at least, a heavy reliance on individual attention may have undesirable consequences. If individual attention is not to be aligned with its concomitant, individual neglect, it seems an opportune time to take a closer look at the method and explore more fully the ways in which it could be further improved.

5

Groups

Once upon a time the idea that children should sit in rows was so deeply ingrained that desks were actually bolted to the floor, thereby completely blocking all possibility of teacher innovation. This rigid pattern was part of a style of teaching in which children were expected to focus, quite literally, on the teacher unless directed otherwise. Rows made it easy for the teacher to monitor what was happening and to ensure that everybody conformed. And for the children the straight lines of desks seemed to reinforce the general message: look ahead and ignore everyone and everything except the teacher and what she is doing. As one commentator has pointed out the children in this type of classroom are jammed together so tightly that psychological escape, much less physical separation, is impossible. And whereas the child's world at eye level is cluttered, disorganised and full of people's shoulders, heads and body movements, the teacher has a clear view of what is going on and sees order and organisation and any deviations from it (Sommer, 1969).

Traditional row lay-outs frequently go hand-in-hand with a teacher-dominated teaching style in which the teacher talks and the children listen. One of the pioneers of classroom observation research who trained observers to use a specially constructed observation schedule to record what classroom life was like, was able to record some of his findings in his now famous 'Rule of two-thirds'. This states that in the typical American classroom (the data were collected from both elementary and secondary classes) someone is talking two-thirds of the time. Two-thirds of the talking is done by the teacher and two-thirds of the time the teacher is talking she is concerned with direct influence, that is to say with lecturing, giving directions or criticising or justifying authority (Amidon and Giammatteo, 1967). This style of teaching has a long history. Montessori, for instance, gave a graphic if rather more emotive description of what classroom life could be like in her times: 'The children, seated, listen motionless hour after hour. When they draw, they have to reproduce another drawing exactly. When they move, it is in obedience to an order given by another person. Their personalities are appraised solely by the standard of passive obedience' (Montessori, 1965).

There can be few British primary classrooms left today where this kind of teacher-dominated atmosphere prevails to such a degree. One of the more obvious manifestations of change is the appearance of new items of classroom furniture and the rearrangement of children into small groups. In newly equipped schools, tables and table units, together with chests of drawers or locker units for children's belongings, often replace the old-fashioned desks with lids and storage wells.

However, new designs of classroom furniture and equipment have followed rather than prompted the move towards group lay-outs. When 189 junior teachers in two L.E.A.s reported how they organised their classrooms in a questionnaire survey, only a small proportion were equipped with modern tables or table units and yet about four teachers out of five had adopted a group lay-out. They had simply pushed together the traditional single and double desks with which they were supplied. The same survey found that group work, defined in terms of children sitting and working together on the same task, was also much in evidence (Bealing, 1972). Group seating arrangements and group work seem to be widely regarded as part of the core of good primary practice. Why is this so?

The explanation is not simple. The widespread change to informal group lay-outs and the strategy of having different groups of children work at different tasks must be seen as part of the general trend towards a more child-centred pedagogy, a development which was both endorsed and encouraged by the Plowden Report (1967). It is interesting to note that although the architectural drawings in the Report show small group seating plans and the merits of group learning are discussed, the relative advantages of different kinds of class-room lay-outs were not singled out for detailed discussion. The emphasis was on flexibility rather than on the assets and drawbacks of particular strategies. As an aside it is worth while pointing out that this notion of flexibility has contributed to the controversial idea that it is not even necessary to provide every child with a seat. However, an illuminating study of a new open-plan primary school which tried a 60 per cent seating level found that within a term all the teachers had built it up to at least 100 per cent. For these teachers, at least, the experiment failed but they did learn a great deal about the relationship between teaching methods and seating requirements in the process. There was no return to class teaching (Hamilton, 1977).

At this stage it is essential to emphasise a warning made earlier in Chapter 1, namely that the outward signs of classroom organisation may give a very misleading impression of what life in that classroom is really like. The presence of new equipment and furniture and small, informally arranged clusters of children is no guarantee that the teacher uses any form of group work very often or that she spends much time actually talking to small groups of children in preference to class instruction or private individual attention. A small American study brought out this point quite sharply. The researcher compared activities in traditional classrooms with those in newer, larger classrooms with portable furniture and concluded that on the whole the teaching pattern was the same and persisted, except in a few instances, regardless of differences in classroom size, features, equipment or design. Interestingly enough, however, the teachers in the newer, larger classrooms liked their classroom environment and believed it made a difference: 'They appreciated their classrooms as comfortable, inspirational places to teach. Their classrooms made them feel that there was no limit to what they could do if they desired'. The real rub came, though, when the teachers emphasised that the larger class-rooms had not changed their teaching methods! (Rolfe, 1961, quoted by Sommer, 1969).

What is the reasoning behind small classroom groups? The Plowden Report arguments are all related to the notion of group learning. Although this term is not actually defined, the Report implies that group learning takes place if a group of children are engaged on a joint project or if they help each other with their own separate pieces of work. It also occurs when the teacher attends to a small group of children together rather than addressing the whole class or coping with children privately one at a time (paras. 755, 757, 758 and 759). Building on the Plowden Report's description it is fair to say that during group learning children are generally clustered together round the teacher or are based at a table or work bench or activity area. However, the key property of this type of learning is not the physical proximity of group members (two children measuring the playground with a tape may be a hundred metres apart) nor the existence of a single joint task necessitating the involvement of all the group members (although this may exist). Its distinguishing feature is the interaction which takes place within the group, both with the teacher and amongst the children when the teacher is absent. Small group classroom lay-outs foster opportunities for interactions of these kinds. The physical appearance of the classroom alone makes it easier for the teacher to think of the class in smaller teaching units and to talk privately to small numbers of children at a time. Furthermore children's physical proximity within the group, especially where their work is the same, is conducive to conversation amongst the group members.

The Plowden Report's arguments for group learning are based on the assumption that the group's interactions, both with the teacher and amongst its members, facilitate a wide range of learning. For instance, following on from the observation that groups were normal, it contended that they provided a milieu which heightened children's self-awareness and sensitivity to others:

> Children of junior school age tend naturally to go about in small groups. Groups of three to 15 pupils are good for many kinds of school work. In this way children learn to get along together, to help one another, and realise their own strengths and weaknesses, as well as those of others. (para. 757)

Furthermore the Report went on to imply that groups can provide a stimulus to children's intellectual and language development:

> [Children] make their meaning clearer to themselves by having to explain it to others ... Some children are so timid and inarticulate that they need to hear their companions put to teachers the questions they themselves are unable to frame ... Able children benefit from being caught up in the thrust and counter thrust of conversation in a small group of children similar to themselves. (para. 757)

The value of group work in mathematics and

science was singled out for special mention:

> Group work has often demonstrated the capacity
> of primary school children to plan and follow up
> mathematical and scientific enquiries. They are
> less shy of risking a hypothesis in a group than
> before the whole class, and sometimes the extrava-
> gant guess turns out to be right. More children,
> too, get the chance of discussing, and so under-
> standing more clearly, what their problem is.
> (para. 758)

The Report made its appraisal of the value of
group learning in the context of the problem of
sharing out the teacher's time if the teacher was to
try to cater to individual needs. Only seven or eight
minutes a day would be available for each child, if
all teaching were individual.

> Teachers, therefore, have to economise by teach-
> ing together a small group of children who are
> roughly at the same stage. Ideally, they might be
> better taught individually, but they gain more
> from a longer period of their teacher's attention,
> even though it is shared with others, than they
> would from a few minutes of individual help.
> This is particularly true of children who have
> reached the same stage in reading and compu-
> tation. A group of this kind should be formed for a
> particular purpose, and should disappear when
> the purpose is achieved. (para. 755)

The authors of the Report were adamant, however,
that groups should not be used for permanent
streaming within the class (para. 824).

These three different lines of reasoning—the need for pragmatism, the stimulus to cognitive and language learning, the opportunity for socio-personal development — add up to a fairly strong endorsement of the merits of group learning. Not that the authors of the Plowden Report were unaware of possible drawbacks. For instance, they point out that it is rare to find a class which fits tidily into groups and whilst apathetic children may be infected by the enthusiasm of others they may sit back as idle passengers, a danger which the teacher needs to watch (paras. 755 and 757). However, their message is clear enough: groups can enable children to 'gain from opportunities to teach as well as to learn' (para. 757).

To what extent do these various claims stand up to test? How realistic are the aspirations? The rest of this chapter will focus on these questions and tap two different sources of information about how groups operate. The first is that of small group ecology, the study of how small groups operate in natural settings. The second is the observational study of classrooms run along group lines. The investigation of how groups function has long fascinated social psychologists but most of their work has been carried out on adults in laboratory experiments (Argyle, 1967). The extent to which their findings apply to children in ordinary class-rooms is a moot point. None the less the traditional type of questions social psychologists ask are highly pertinent. For instance, how are children's contacts with each other affected by such things as the size of the group, its composition and the type of task being undertaken? It seems highly probable that an understanding of these kinds of influences is essential for laying the foundations of successful group work in the classroom. It is therefore very unfortunate that so little is known about the dynamics of classroom groups, about what makes for effective interaction. The study of groups in any kind of natural setting is in its infancy. Nevertheless the small amount of available evidence shows there is no room for complacency.

Consider first the question of how many children make a viable group. The Plowden Report recommended the use of groups containing up to fifteen children although, if one survey is anything to go by, teachers seem to like medium-sized groups of five to eight children (Bealing, 1972). Is this just a convenient administrative number or is it also the size most conducive to the types of interaction needed for group learning? A pioneer study of people engaged in face-to-face interaction, conducted more than twenty-five years ago in two American cities, hints that medium-sized groups may be too large from the children's point of view (James, 1951). When natural groupings of work people, pedestrians, shoppers, participants at public gatherings and children playing were observed, it turned out that almost three-quarters of all these groups contained just two people. Another fifth contained only three. It would appear, then, that in many ordinary situations people prefer the physical and psychological intimacy of groups of two or, at most, three. Does this apply to classroom groups as well? If, for example, there are six children with the same task sitting at a table do they tend to split into twos and threes when interacting? If so it is easy to see how the amount and range of contact the teacher hopes for may be drastically reduced.

Of course group size is not the only factor which may influence the pattern of interaction, of who talks how much to whom. There is also the question of group composition. Some teachers allow their class a large measure of free choice as to where they sit and work and yet others have quite elaborate strategies, changing perhaps for different activities, for working out who sits and works where and when. They may, for instance, try to mix boys and girls, balance good or poor readers or concentrate children at a similar stage together. Such strategies are based on the expectation that when children are congregated together in this fashion, with a joint task or similar work, they will interact with each other in ways which are conducive to group learning. However, children may feel ill-at-ease with particular members of their group and opt out of any contact at all. The teacher's plans to bring about the range of contact she wants between different group members could be thwarted very easily.

These concerns about the size and composition of classroom groups seem warranted in view of the findings which emerged from an exploratory study of pupil behaviour in six informal junior school classrooms in this country (Boydell, 1975). The children were informally arranged in small groups, working at mathematics. Six observers, who were themselves teachers, were trained to use an observation schedule which focused on children's classroom activities. They visited each of the six classrooms in turn and were accompanied by another observer using a second observation instrument which focused on the teacher. This teacher schedule, and the information it yielded, have already been discussed in Chapter 4.

The observers using the pupil schedule watched individual children in the classroom one after another in a pre-arranged and arbitrary order, coding each child's behaviour five times at twenty-five-second intervals. The number of categories coded depended on what the child was doing. Three categories were coded if the child was not interacting, nine were coded if he was interacting with one or more of his classmates and seven were coded if he was interacting with the teacher. All in all this method of multiple coding provided a great mass of information on how children spent their time.

The findings about children's interactions with each other confirmed the fact that grouping a particular set of children together is no guarantee that they will freely interact. In the first place more than 90 per cent of the observed interaction involved only two children. This seems to confirm that children in classrooms, like the city dwellers mentioned earlier, tend to prefer pairs. Furthermore four-fifths of all the interaction was between children of the same sex. Admittedly some of the children were based at single-sex tables but the proportion still exceeded three-quarters when the interactions of children belonging to mixed groups of boys and girls was examined. The observed sex bias is potentially serious because it militates against group discussions involving boys and girls and is a good example of how group composition can influence the interaction pattern which occurs. Moreover it can exacerbate the difficulties caused by children's apparent dislike of talking or working with more than one other child. As an example consider the situation where a teacher wants children to help a boy with reading difficulties to cope with his work cards. She might position the boy at a table with two girls who like each other and are proficient readers. Her plans, however, could come to naught. As children tend to prefer contact with just one other child at a time, preferably of the same sex as themselves, it would not be at all surprising if the two girls communicated with each other and excluded the boy. Under these circumstances the chances that children will 'learn to get along together, to help one another and realise their own strengths and weaknesses, as well as those of others', (Plowden Report, para. 757) seem very remote indeed.

The size and sex mix of groups are just two of the more obvious ways in which groups can differ. How is the interaction pattern affected by the two popular ploys of mixing (or concentrating) children at different stages? Or by setting up multiracial groups? Or by mixing children of different personality types or from different kinds of home background? Unfortunately very little is known, but the mass of research into the dynamics of small groups of adults in laboratory experiments, together with the small amount of available evidence on children's groups, suggests that the processes at work may be very subtle and far more complex than is sometimes appreciated.

The type of task the children work at may also be very important. Laboratory experiments with small groups of adults have shown that performance is superior if the group task requires joint effort (Deutsch, 1949). Furthermore they have also shown that the nature of the task determines who is most influential: changes of task can lead to changes of leadership within the group (Argyle, 1967).

A study conducted in the U.S.A. showed that different kinds of task even influenced where pairs of children wanted to sit! When engaged in a cooperative activity it turned out that both pre-school children and nine- to twelve-year-olds tended to sit side by side. However, when competing they positioned themselves across a corner and when working separately on their own tasks they used more distant arrangements. Girls sat side by side more often than boys. Interestingly enough the face-to-face position, which is commonly preferred by adults, was only rarely chosen by young children (Norum, Russo and Sommer, 1967). However, another study showed that as children grew older face-to-face arrangements increased in popularity and side by side seating fell off (Elkin, 1964, quoted by Sommer, 1969). It would therefore seem worth while for the teacher to pay some attention to who sits where within a group and to respond to children's preferences for different kinds of arrangements for different kinds of work. For instance, if she wanted two children to have a go at some cooperative venture she might be wise to encourage them to sit side by side rather than take up competing positions across the corner of the table. Moreover she may also find it worthwhile to consider her own physical positioning when helping children at their tables. Do they feel more comfortable if she sits down beside them?

Sitting down with a group can, incidentally, prove a most illuminating experience especially if the teacher takes a non-directive role. It is, in fact, probably the only way in which the teacher can tell whether her various decisions on group size, composition and task are having their planned effect on what children do and say and learn. The following vignette illustrates quite sharply the insights to be gained from simply sitting and watching a group at work (Worthington, 1969).

A group of two boys and two girls, all eight-year-olds, were set a task involving the weighing of small wooden blocks, of three different sizes, into mixed one-pound lots. They were then asked to produce half-pound lots, but were provided with only one set of scales and a one-pound weight. The two boys took possession of the scales, and set about the first part of the task with enthusiasm. This job was quickly done, and they moved on to the second task with a great show of industry, but with little understanding, and met with no success. The writer was acting as a participant observer for this work, and he quietly suggested to one of the girls that she should try to solve the problem. She quickly declined, with some embarrassment, although it was fairly obvious that she understood what was involved. The boys were soon frustrated by their unsuccessful attempts to solve the problem by trial and error methods, and readily agreed to the observer's suggestion, to them, that the girls should be allowed to try to solve the problem. They pushed the scales and blocks across to the girls with derisive glee, and obviously considered the idea of the girls attempting a problem that they had failed to solve to be quite ludicrous. The girls immediately performed the correct operations and were successful at the first attempt. They appeared to have complete insight into the problem. Their result was immediately challenged by the boys, who demanded replication of the operations, and accused the girls of cheating. The girls capitulated under the hostile pressure, abandoned the technique of adding blocks to the scales in pairs (to permit subsequent even division), and failed to repeat their previous success. The boys were delighted, the girls relieved, and normal role relationships restored. (page 95)

How typical is this kind of thing? As there is very little detailed information about how natural classroom groups operate it is rather difficult to assess. However, it is probably true to say that there may be quite a large gap between what a group is really up to and what the teacher thinks and hopes is happening. Clearly the quality of group interaction is at least as important as its quantity and the number of children involved.

One clue to the quality of group interaction is the amount of sustained work-oriented contact. In the study of children's behaviour in six informal junior classrooms, which was referred to earlier, children interacted with each other for about a third of the time (Boydell, 1975). However, on average only slightly more than a third of this interaction was sustained in the sense that it bridged the gap to the next time of recording twenty-five seconds later.

Sustained work-oriented contact only accounted for a small proportion of each lesson. This seems to suggest that extended conversations in which children explain and develop their ideas and arguments may be relatively uncommon. Furthermore it also throws considerable doubt on the extent to which groups, in reality, provide children 'with opportunities to teach as well as to learn' (Plowden Report, 1967, para. 757). Of course this is not to say that sustained work-oriented contacts never occur and that it is inherently impossible to set up groups from which children profit. However, it would seem that the creation and supervision of interacting groups requires a great amount of teacher skill. It might also be true to add that, in the face of a multitude of conflicting demands on the teacher's time and energies, the magnitude and importance of this management task is often underestimated. In the study of six informal classrooms, where children sitting together sometimes had the same task, teachers rarely took the opportunity for talking to a group. By and large they much preferred to give private individual attention (Boydell, 1974). This is a costly method in terms of the teacher's resources (see Chapter 4). Furthermore, if groups are to function effectively, it may be up to the teacher to give a lead by instructing children in groups. In this way children may come to learn that the teacher thinks of them together and wants them to cooperate with each other.

Unfortunately the enthusiasm of teachers who want to make a group approach work, not just for reasons of administrative convenience but because of a deep-seated belief in the more fundamental values of group learning, is not encouraged by critics who use findings such as those reported here to point a reproachful and accusing finger at what these teachers are trying to do. Even those who may be sympathetic to the idea of group learning may be uncommitted in practice. Look, they say, at those children who never learn to write properly because they have a sideways view of the teacher's hand-writing on the blackboard. Look at children's feeble efforts to decipher and copy the work of children sitting opposite with 'p's written as 'd's and vice versa. Look at the opportunity small groups provide for chatter and how on earth can the teacher tell, as she scans the room, when any given conversation is to do with work and when it is not?

The study of six informal classrooms mentioned previously threw some light on these kinds of question. It found that the typical child was only physically near the teacher, or receiving any kind of contact from her on his own or as a group or class member, for rather less than a fifth of the time. Never-theless children were involved in their work for two-thirds of the time. This figure rose to above seven-tenths when the time spent waiting to see the teacher was included. In view of the relatively low amount of adult contact of any kind these findings provide ample evidence that children in informal groupings have a considerable ability to remain work-oriented with a minimum of direct ongoing supervision (Boydell, 1975).

The same study also compared how work-oriented children were when they were interacting with each other and when they were on their own, neither interacting amongst themselves nor with the teacher. When children were alone they were involved with their work or waiting to see the teacher for about four-fifths of the time. However, when they were interacting with each other the figure dropped to less than half. Clearly, then, there is some substance to the claim that children are more likely to be time-wasting when they are interacting than when they are not. Nevertheless it must be remembered that even though children had opportunities to interact with each other, they remained alone for most of the time. Time-wasting through chatter only accounted for a small proportion of the lesson as a whole.

Furthermore there was no evidence to support the widespread belief that the more children interact with each other the more likely it becomes that their conversation has nothing to do with work. Indeed in this particular set of six classrooms a detailed analysis showed quite the converse to be true. Although in each classroom work involvement was always lower when children were interacting than when they were not, there was a positive relationship between the total percentage of pupil-pupil interaction and the percentage of work-oriented activity during this interaction. Put another way, the greater the amount of observed contact, the more likely it was that the contact was work-oriented. The classroom with the greatest amount of pupil-pupil contact (40 per cent of observed lesson time) recorded the highest amount of work-oriented interaction (57 per cent of observed pupil-pupil contact time). One likely explanation is that the teacher concerned, by dint of skilled management, had taught his class how to work in groups. Classroom chatter and time-wasting need not be synonymous.

All the evidence suggests that successful group learning does not just happen spontaneously given certain organisational arrangements. How to work successfully in groups seems to be a skill which children (like adults) must learn. How to set up and sustain a successful group approach seems to be a skill which teachers must develop. It involves the ability to mesh a deep understanding of what makes groups work with a thorough knowledge of the needs of individual children. There are probably no short cuts.

6

The Self-fulfilling Prophecy

It is a well-known fact that children from low social class backgrounds often perform poorly at school. Of course there are numerous exceptions but these do little to alter the widespread expectation, backed up by numerous research studies, that children from working class families are far less likely to achieve as much at school as children from middle class homes. Why should this be so? One argument that is sometimes advanced is that working class children are inherently less bright. However, such a view begs all kinds of questions about the nature of intelligence. Although the available evidence makes it hard to deny that heredity has an influence it also shows that environmental factors have a significant impact (Pidgeon, 1970). Intelligence is now widely regarded as the product of a complex and subtle interaction between heredity and environment which makes it extraordinarily difficult, if not impossible, to disentangle the separate effects of each. Nevertheless the nature-nurture debate remains highly controversial and tends to obscure one very straightforward point: it is quite possible to acknowledge that there may be biological limits to intelligence in the population as a whole and, at the same time, to give wholehearted support to the removal of constraints which seem to be working against the interests of children from low social class backgrounds.

A great deal of effort has been expended in an attempt to discover what these environmental constraints might be. One widely accepted conclusion is that some of the major causes of low achievement lie in children's early upbringing. The damage has been done, so the argument runs, before children enter school. And even nursery education may come too late. All the teacher can do is try to compensate, as best she can, for the supposed deficiencies in her charges' early years. Accusing fingers are pointed at the nature of children's language experience, their inability to postpone short-term gratification of goals for more long-term objectives, their lack of encouragement from home to work hard at school and aspire to higher-status jobs than their parents, their unfamiliarity with the essentially middle class mores and norms of school. Of course not all teachers subscribe to these kinds of explanations and a growing number of commentators have been challenging the assumptions on which the opinions are based. Controversy abounds. This makes it all the more important not to lose sight of one important point. However pervasive the influence of the home (and no-one would deny its effect is strong although the precise way it works is still unclear) children spend a large portion of their lives at school. There is a growing body of research evidence which supports the common sense supposition that teachers *do* make a difference (Good, Biddle and Brophy, 1975). The key issue is not whether teachers have an impact on children but rather how that influence works and how its effect could be enhanced. It may well be that teachers could make a significant contribution to solving the problem of low-achieving children if they had the answers to those particular questions.

How one person influences another person to think, feel and act in certain ways lies at the very core of human relationships and hence of teaching. Given the likelihood that the processes at work when teachers and children interact are highly complex and partly unconscious, it is hardly surprising that the teacher-pupil relationship has proved very difficult to explore. None the less there is no shortage of theories and one, in particular, has attracted a great deal of publicity. This is the notion of the self-fulfilling prophecy.

The Concise Oxford Dictionary defines a prophecy as the 'foretelling of future events'. A self-fulfilling prophecy is one in which the very act of foretelling somehow makes it more likely that the predicted events will occur. A trivial example of the self-fulfilling prophecy in everyday life is when someone fears a mishap on account of fatigue, starts worrying about this possibility instead of concentrating on the job in hand and then actually has an accident. The accident in its turn confirms the accuracy of the original foreboding.

Put like this it is easy to retort that prophecies, particularly self-fulfilling ones, are too infrequent to be of much consequence, educational or otherwise. Although it is probably true that people are rarely aware of making predictions about how other people will react or behave there is a great deal of evidence from social psychology that, consciously or not, people bring all kinds of expectations into human encounters. In one classic study students were led to believe either that a 'guest lecturer' would be a warm type of person or that he would be cold. Although all the students saw the same man those who expected him to be warm rated him as more considerate of others, informal, sociable, popular and humorous than those who expected him to be cold. In addition more of those expecting him to be warm participated in the discussion. This study clearly demonstrated that expectations can influence the impressions and behaviour of the people who hold them (Kelley, 1950). But can these impressions and behaviour influence other people in such a way that they confirm the original expectations held about them? In a word, can expectations lead on to a self-fulfilling prophecy? And does this also happen in classrooms?

In 1968, at a time in the U.S.A. when great amounts of faith and energy were being invested in the idea that education could go a long way to redressing the social and political injustices of American society, two researchers published a book which claimed to show that the self-fulfilling prophecy did indeed exist in American classrooms (Rosenthal and Jacobson, 1968). Called *Pygmalion in the Classroom* it reported the results of an investigation which seemed to prove that teachers' expectations influenced pupils' intellectual development. And it did not require much imagination to go one step further and claim that the self-fulfilling prophecy was a major reason why children from low social class backgrounds did poorly at school. The teacher, through her professional studies and personal experience, has come to expect that children from low socio-economic groups will not achieve as much at school as children from higher social classes. Consequently she treats children differently on the basis of the sort of home she thinks they come from. Different treatment gives rise to different levels of academic performance which proves to the teacher that she was right in the first place. Such a plausible yet contentious idea was almost bound to cause a furore. Small wonder that *Pygmalion in the Classroom* became the centre of a storm.

Before evaluating the study it is first necessary to look briefly at what was done. In May of the 1964 school year, children attending a streamed elementary school with a predominantly low socio-economic intake were given an intelligence test, containing verbal and reasoning sub-tests. Eighteen classes covering a six-year age span were involved. Twenty per cent of the children in the school were then selected at random. At the beginning of the next school year their teachers were told that the test of intellectual blooming (which was really the intelligence test) had predicted that these children would show great academic gains during the school year. In January and May 1965 the children were again tested on the same intelligence test and all those remaining in the school were followed up and tested yet again in May of the following year. The results seemed sensational. Although the groups of 'bloomers' and undesignated children had both gained I.Q. points when the major testing took place in the first May, the 'bloomers' (who were really, of course, selected at random) gained significantly more I.Q. points on the total test and also on the reasoning test (although no differences were found for the verbal sub-test). Equally striking was the fact that the greatest differences occurred with the youngest children.

Unfortunately this ambitious attempt to provide empirical evidence for the self-fulfilling prophecy with primary children cannot be taken at face value. The experimental design is riddled with flaws and prompted one commentator to write that the study was 'so defective technically that one can only regret that it ever got beyond the eyes of the original investigators!' (Thorndike, 1968). The problems begin with the particular intelligence test used which is quite inadequate for young children and children from low socio-economic backgrounds, precisely those for which the most dramatic results emerged. This may explain some of the extraordinary I.Q. scores reported which were at the 'imbecile' and 'low moron' level. Furthermore the tests were administered by teachers and it is not known whether they were trained to give the test in a standardised way to make it fair for all the children. In addition quite a number of children were lost to the study but this problem is ignored. If they were lost unevenly from different years or sub-groups or ability ranges the results may have been different. Another major weakness was that most of the teachers said that they paid little or no attention to the lists of 'bloomers' they had been given. Out of seventy-two 'bloomers' teachers were only able to recall the names of eighteen. It seems highly improbable that teachers expected different performance from the children designated as 'bloomers' if they did not know or could not remember who they were. And if all these problems are not enough there are a large number of important criticisms about how the raw data were processed statistically and how the results were reported (Snow, 1969; Thorndike, 1968).

Despite its multitude of serious shortcomings the study had one very desirable effect: it stirred the imagination of many other investigators. A great deal of research, mainly in the U.S.A., has followed Rosenthal and Jacobson's pioneering but flawed initiative. Although most of the subsequent work has failed to demonstrate the teacher expectancy effect (or has been inconclusive because of inadequate research designs) a few studies have clearly demonstrated the effect of teacher bias. These more promising investigations have moved away from efforts to see whether manipulated teacher expectations affected children's I.Q. Instead they have used far more sophisticated approaches, involving, for instance, teachers' own naturally occurring expectations, records of teachers' class-room behaviour and tests of children's attainment on specific criteria rather than a global measure of I.Q.

One study, for example, showed conclusively that teachers' own long-established opinions can affect the level of reading success of six- to seven-year-olds. Boys taught by teachers who believed that boys would not read as well as girls did worse than the girls taught by the same teachers. Furthermore they did worse than both the girls and the boys taught by teachers who believed that boys would read as well as girls (Palardy, 1969).

A second study threw some light on how teachers' expectations were actually communicated by observing graduate education students work individually with a single child for a ten-minute period (Beez, 1968). The task consisted of twenty symbols like 'STOP' and 'DANGER', each printed on a separate card, and the aim was to teach as many symbols as possible in the time available. The children were tested afterwards. Each teacher was given a faked psychological evaluation of the child they were to teach. All the evaluations contained identical data but these were presented positively if the child was said to have 'high ability' and negatively if the child was said to have 'low ability'. In fact whether a child received a positive or negative evaluation was simply a matter of luck: before the experiment began half the children had been quite arbitrarily labelled 'high ability' and half had been labelled 'low ability'. It turned out that children who had received the positive evaluations learnt more symbols and were treated differently by their teachers. The teachers attempted to teach them more symbols, explained the meaning of a word less often, gave fewer examples and spent more time on the task itself as against other matters. Only one teacher thought the task to be too difficult for the pupil. By contrast, two-thirds of the teachers with the negatively evaluated children thought the task to be beyond their grasp. Given the liking for private individual attention in British classrooms this study highlights a number of traps of which the teacher should be aware.

Another investigation focused in even greater detail on how teachers communicated their expectations when giving children individual attention, although not necessarily in private (Brophy and Good, 1970). At the start of the study four teachers from one school, all with six- to seven-year-olds, ranked the children in their class in order of achievement. The three boys and three girls at the top of the list, together with the three boys and three girls at the bottom, were then singled out for further investigation although the teachers were not told who was being studied. For two whole mornings and two afternoons observers recorded all the interactions which took place between these children and their teachers using a specially designed observation instrument. In addition to being observed the children were also given an achievement test at the end of the year.

The results were striking. Not only were the teachers' subjective rankings of children's achievements accurate when compared to the objective test results but the classroom activity of children rated high on their list differed in a number of important respects from the behaviour of those rated low. The children rated high raised their hands more often, initiated more procedural and work-related interactions, received less criticism of their behaviour, gave more correct answers, made fewer partially correct, incorrect or 'don't know' responses and had fewer reading problems overall and fewer per turn when called upon to read. Even more interesting were the differences in how teachers handled the responses of the children they saw as high and low achievers. They gave the high achievers a greater percentage of praise following a correct answer and a smaller amount of criticism (coupled to a greater percentage of repetitions or rephrasings) following a wrong answer. The high achievers also received a higher percentage of repetitions, rephrasings and clues following reading problems and were far less likely to have their answers ignored by the teacher. As the investigators say the findings 'show that the teachers consistently favored the highs over the lows in demanding and reinforcing quality performance'.

Were these teachers aware that they were discriminating against low achievers in these ways? The answer is almost certainly no. Although there is nothing very remarkable in the fact that different children were handled in different ways (indeed, this is the whole point of individual attention) it is hard to believe that any teacher would consciously give low achievers less encouragement than high achievers. The possibility of unconscious bias makes the findings all the more worrying. It also makes it all the more important to find out how different expectations arise. How do different children pick up the labels of high, average and low ability?

Unfortunately there is as yet no clear-cut answer. The process almost certainly involves the complex interaction of teachers' and children's personalities within the classroom. It is most unlikely that teacher expectations arise from a single pupil or teacher characteristic. It is far more probable that a number of factors work together to produce in the teacher's mind the idea that a certain pupil will or will not be an academic high-flier, or will or will not be a behaviour problem. A number of studies have suggested what some of these characteristics might be (Grieger, 1971).

One important factor, for instance, seems to be the

child's sex. There is a lot of evidence which suggests that the widespread view that girls achieve more and behave better than boys is objectively quite correct (Brophy and Good, 1970). In particular boys are more disruptive in the classroom and receive more disciplinary contacts. Now it is possible to argue that differences in child upbringing and so forth mean that boys are more difficult to control at school and that boys therefore bring the teacher's disapproval on themselves quite independently of any teacher bias. But is this the whole picture? If the teacher expects boys to behave poorly might this not lead to a chain of events in which any bad behaviour which might have arisen anyway is unconsciously aggravated? This certainly seems a possibility worth considering.

The way children go about their classroom activities in all the different kinds of situations which arise is another factor which seems to influence teacher expectations about what they will achieve. One study has looked specifically at the influence of kindergarten children's behavioural style in the classroom on the teachers' appraisal of their intelligence. After nearly a year's contact with the children, teachers were asked to characterise their style in terms of the quality of their participation in new activities and situations in the classroom. Four categories of participation were defined: 'plungers', 'go-alongers', 'sideliners' and 'non-participators'. The teachers also rated each child's intelligence and it appeared that this was greatly influenced by their classroom style. For example, of the six children whose real intelligence, as measured on an objective test the following autumn, was overestimated, five had been classified as 'plungers' (Gordon and Thomas, 1967). Obviously children's classroom behaviour is a rich source of information to the teacher. Often it is only by watching him work and talk and respond to her and his classmates that she can find out how best to help him. However, this investigation shows how necessary it is to check out these impressions constantly, both against each other and with other sources of information where available. Failure to do so may result in invalid perceptions and expectations which work to the detriment of some children.

The socio-economic class of children's home backgrounds is a third factor which has attracted considerable interest as a likely influence on teachers' expectations. Indeed the disappointing attainments of working class children is the main reason why the whole notion of the self-fulfilling prophecy has attracted so much attention. However, it is one thing to say that children do poorly partly because they are labelled working class and quite another thing to say how they came to be so designated in the first place. The teacher has direct knowledge of a child's sex and his way of operating in the classroom. With social class, however, she often has to make inferences. How does this labelling, with its attendant expectations, get established? How does the teacher communicate these expectations to the children concerned? One famous American study focused on these questions of how teachers formulated and communicated expectations based on their perceptions of children's socio-economic class (Rist, 1970).

The investigator traced what happened to a group

of black children in an urban ghetto school from the time they began kindergarten to part-way through their third year. On the eighth day of school the kindergarten teacher made permanent seating arrangements. She placed the children at three tables. Those at Table 1 she thought of as the 'fast learners' whereas she commented that some of those placed at Table 2 and most of those at Table 3 'at times seem to have no idea of what is going on in the classroom'. It is extremely important to note that all these evaluative judgements about children's likely potential, and the consequent grouping, had been made subjectively by one teacher in the absence of any formal assessment of their academic capacity when the children were only eight days into their school career.

The criteria the teacher used for deciding who was a fast learner seemed to be based on the values of her own middle class background. Her 'ideal' successful child seemed to be the one with highly prized middle class attributes — ease of interaction with adults, ease of conversation in standard American English, the ability to become a leader, a neat and clean appearance, the ability to participate well as a group member and a family that is educated, employed, living together and interested in the child. Children showing these attributes found themselves labelled as fast learners on Table 1. Children not appearing to possess the criteria which the teacher considered essential for success found themselves labelled failures and were relegated to Tables 2 and 3. The organisation of the classroom into these three groups on the eighth day subsequently became the basis of differential treatment of the children for the rest of the year: the teacher concentrated on the fast learners.

This had repercussions on the children's behaviour. For a start the fast learners at Table 1 ridiculed and belittled the children at Tables 2 and 3. Secondly they sought solidarity and closeness with the teacher and urged the other children to comply with her wishes. It was as though they perceived the lower esteem which the teacher ascribed to the rest of the class and realised that they held a higher status in the teacher's eyes. By contrast the two major responses of the children at Tables 2 and 3 to isolation from the teacher and ridicule from their classmates were withdrawal and in-group hostility. Some of their aggressive behaviour mirrored what the teacher and other children were saying about them. For example there were numerous occasions when these Table 2 and 3 children called each other stupid. Racial overtones, physical threats and even spitting were also noted. Significantly, none of these children had begun the year by ridiculing each other.

In this classroom, at least, the evidence suggests that the teacher had unwittingly set in motion a series of events that would ensure that her fast learners would succeed and the remainder would fail. When the eighteen children who remained in the school moved up to a new teacher at the beginning of the next school year they again found themselves divided into three groups, this time called Tables A, B and C in descending order of merit. Hardly surprisingly no Table 2 or 3 child won promotion to Table A. Quite apart from anything else the kindergarten teacher's disproportionate allocation of teaching time meant that only the old Table 1 children had completed the kindergarten work and were ready to move on. The rest had to spend the first few weeks of the new year finishing it off. A similar grouping pattern recurred once more when the children moved up a second time into their third year. This time the three groups had names. The top group were designated 'Tigers', the intermediate group were called 'Cardinals' and, as if to reinforce their low status, the bottom group were named 'Clowns'. None of the children who had been on Tables B and C the year before moved up to the 'Tigers'.

It is all too easy to argue that what happens to children in an American inner area school, where teachers were practising such blatant forms of classroom streaming, bears little resemblance to children's primary school experience in this country. However, a number of investigations in British classrooms have pointed to the possible influence of teachers' attitudes and expectations on children's learning. There is no room for complacency.

The National Foundation for Educational Research (N.F.E.R.) study of primary school French discovered that low-ability children who performed badly on both general attainment tests and an aural French test tended to be concentrated in a small number of schools where the heads had expressed hostility to teaching French to low-ability children. By contrast those children who performed badly on the general attainment tests but scored above average on the French test tended to be found in schools where the head had expressed more favourable attitudes. As the attitudes of heads and teachers were closely linked within each school it seems that the teachers' expectations may well have influenced children's achievements (Burstall, 1970).

Another N.F.E.R. study focused on the teaching of reading in infant schools. It found a rather disturbing discrepancy between teachers' evaluations of children's reading ability based on the level of the book they had reached, and children's actual tested performance. The teachers' assessments showed that children in middle class and upper working class areas read much better than those in lower working class areas, with the children from middle class homes doing best of all. However, the superiority of the middle class pupils did not show up when their reading was tested objectively: although lower working class pupils were still markedly inferior, upper working class pupils were doing better than they were being credited. Further investigation showed, amongst other things, that various factors seemed to influence teachers' perceptions of children's social class. These included conversations, class 'News' and observations of children's clothes and other personal belongings. It turned out that teachers' inferences about children's home backgrounds were least reliable in the lowest social areas. Perhaps just as significantly teachers in lower working class areas, as compared with those in upper working class areas, were more likely to wait for pupils' reading 'readiness' and less likely to provide opportunities for assessing children's perceptual development (Goodacre, 1968).

Another study examined teachers' models of the 'successful' infant school child in two different areas of London. One area was overwhelmingly working class and the other area was overwhelmingly middle class. At the end of the children's first year at school the teachers' model in the working class area stressed children's responsiveness to the teacher's control. This was valued too by teachers in the middle class area but pupils' ability to initiate was seen as equally important. By the time children had reached the end of their second school year the picture had changed. Teachers in the working class area now put more emphasis on pupil-initiating behaviour: the 'successful' infant school child would proffer explanations, ask questions *and* be cooperative, attentive and responsive to being questioned. By contrast teachers in the middle class area were now less likely to want children to initiate *and* be amenable to their control. For them the 'successful' infant school child was, above all, independent. Other factors, too, contributed to the teachers' notions of the 'successful' child. Brightness, for instance, was highly regarded in both areas although children were much more sharply polarised in terms of their measured ability in the working class area. The results suggested that teachers in the two areas held rather different ideas about what makes for 'success' in the infant school child, ideas which may end up as self-fulfilling prophecies if reflected in classroom practice (Brandis and Bernstein, 1974).

Classroom observation of children perceived as having different home backgrounds formed a major ingredient of another fascinating, exploratory investigation (Nash, 1973). Drawing on infor-mation collected in a progressive, unstreamed primary school the investigator found that children the teachers thought came from poor homes did worse than those believed to come from good homes. This finding held regardless of whether attainment was measured on an objective test or was estimated by the teachers. The really key point, however, was that children's actual social class (taken from information on their school records) was not at one with the teachers' perceptions of their home background. Neither was this more objective measure of social class related to the children's academic performance, a finding which is out of line with those from other investigations in this area. Clearly the results from one small case study do not invalidate the well-established tendency for children of low social class origin to do poorly at school. Nevertheless they do hint that teacher expectations, as well as pupils' home backgrounds, may be partly to blame. In this study teachers were so convinced that social class must be important that they perceived the link to exist even when objectively it did not.

For some of the teachers children's perceived social class was one component of how favourably the children were regarded. Needless to say children thought of favourably performed better and had different kinds of classroom encounters with the teacher. The following extracts illustrate the subtle ways in which these encounters could differ. Robert, for instance, was not particularly well regarded by the teacher:

She [the teacher] heads him [Robert] over to the model tray. 'We're going to have the Rockies either side and that's going to be a wee pass. Are

you very good at making mountain shapes?'
Robert looks doubtfully at the heap of papier
mâché. 'No?' asks the teacher. 'Well, I'll get someone else to do that then.' She tells him to do a
picture instead. Robert goes back to his desk. He
looks about, sees that he hasn't any paper to draw
on and decides to finish his English. A couple of
minutes later teacher asks the class, 'Anyone still
doing English?' Robert raises his hand. 'Oh, come
on, Robert,' she says.

Jamie, by contrast, is perceived much more
favourably than Robert. The following account of a
few minutes of Jamie's classroom experiences makes
this abundantly clear:

The class are now given instructions about the
project they are to do. Everybody is going to write
diaries of a Western pioneer family. 'I'm going to
put you in families. Husbands and wives —
there's no need to be silly about it — and children.'
She [their teacher] looks round to see who has
finished the English work. 'Right,' she says,
'Jamie, you pick your waggon.' Jamie grins and
stands up and makes great play over picking his
friends who move over to his desk.

These illustrations highlight the fact that Robert
and Jamie had rather different kinds of relationships with their teacher. Presumably it is these kinds
of differences, as reflected in how the teacher
interacts with individual children, which partly
account for another of this study's interesting
findings. It was discovered that children were very
adept at assessing how good they were at their work

relative to their classmates. Their estimates corresponded closely with the teacher's even when there were no obvious clues like streaming by table. It is therefore possible that the effects of any teacher bias could be compounded by the children themselves. A child who believes he is a failure and is regarded as such by both his teacher and his peers *may* try to improve his performance and his image. Alternatively he may give up completely. Furthermore, being unfavourably perceived may have unfortunate consequences well beyond the primary stage. In a related study children were followed as they made the transition from five feeder primary schools into a single comprehensive school. Significantly those children who found themselves in the remedial class at the end of their first term of secondary education were far more unfavourably perceived by their primary teachers than a group of children of comparably low I.Q. and low class position in the primary school who were not placed in this class.

From this and other studies of the effects of teachers' expectations it is only too easy to conclude that teachers are totally to blame for any self-fulfilling prophecies which arise. However, this ignores the fact that teachers operate within the social context of a school. Teachers may feel professionally autonomous in the classroom (Taylor, Reid, Holley and Exon, 1974) but they work against a background of social constraints like the school ethos with its expectations about how a teacher should teach. It may well be that constraints like these influence what the teacher does in the classroom in ways of which she is not fully aware. For example, where a school adopts an informal approach there are immense problems of control and management for the class teacher, some of which have been described in previous chapters. The teacher has to develop a rationale for sharing out her time and energies. One way is to try to classify children into different levels and to decide who is most likely to benefit from these scarce resources. Evidence for this kind of stratification of children by their teachers was found by investigators who carried out a case study of three infant teachers in a progressive junior mixed and infants' school in England (Sharp and Green, 1975). Faced with the question of what to do with freely choosing children in the classroom all three teachers developed strategies for differentiating amongst them and accorded the successful pupils more and different attention. The researchers argued that the major irony of any classroom requiring both informality and pupil choice is that if all the children are interested, keen and teacher-directed the teacher's management problem would be insuperable. The system only works because many pupils are not like this. Seen in this way, therefore, the school philosophy itself may put pressures on teachers which they can only resolve by developing different levels of expectation and patterns of interaction for different children. Any comprehensive explanation of the origins of the self-fulfilling prophecy must incorporate the possibility of these wider social influences and their relationships to prevailing aims and ideas about 'good' classroom practice.

This chapter has looked at some of the evidence relating to the notion of the self-fulfilling prophecy. There is ample proof that teachers hold differential expectations for different children and there is growing awareness of some of the factors which might influence their judgements, including the school ethos itself. In the case of expectations based on children's perceived socio-economic backgrounds there is even some insight into how they may arise. However, there is no definitive answer as to whether these expectations go on to be self-fulfilling, although there are plenty of clues that suggest that they can (Nash, 1976). For the self-fulfilling prophecy to be confirmed it is necessary to show how different expectations lead to different levels of performance in different children which are in line with the teachers' initial predictions. Very few studies have succeeded in going this far.

Even though the case for the self-fulfilling prophecy is by no means proved there is still sufficient circumstantial evidence for the teacher to treat it as a serious possibility. It may not be as widespread or as important as is sometimes claimed but it may still be operating against the interests of one or more children in her class. Are any of her attitudes and expectations, picked up through reading and personal experience, being unwittingly reflected in the way she treats different children? Are children responding differentially to her as a result, thereby confirming and reinforcing her different expectations for them? Is she quite unconsciously enhancing the performance of those she expects to do well whilst simultaneously depressing the standards of behaviour and work she obtains from those for whom she is not so optimistic? The studies outlined here suggest that it might be wise for the teacher to reflect on these questions.

References *and* Name Index

Adams, R. S., and **Biddle, B. J.** (1970) *Realities of Teaching — Explorations with Video Tape* (New York: Holt, Rinehart and Winston). *71*

Amidon, E., and **Giammatteo, M.** (1967) 'The Verbal Behavior of Superior Elementary Teachers', in Amidon and Hough 1967 (eds), 186-8. *86*

Amidon, E., and **Hough, J. B.** (1967) (eds) *Interaction Analysis: Theory, Research and Application* (Reading, Mass: Addison-Wesley)

Argyle, M. (1967) *The Psychology of Interpersonal Behaviour* (Harmondsworth: Penguin Books). *92, 97*

Ashton, P., Kneen, P., and **Davies, F.** (1975) *Aims into Practice in the Primary School — A Guide for Teachers* (London: University of London Press). *40*

Ashton, P., Kneen, P., Davies, F., and **Holley, B. J.** (1975) *The Aims of Primary Education: A Study of Teachers' Opinions* (London: Macmillan Education). *6, 31, 32, 38, 76*

Barker Lunn, J. C. (1970) *Streaming in the Primary School* (Slough: N.F.E.R.). *46*

Barth, R., and **Rathbone, C.** (1972) 'The Open School: A Way of Thinking about Children, Learning, Knowledge', in Westby-Gibson 1972 (ed), 389-91. *76*

Bealing, D. (1972) 'The Organization of Junior School Classrooms', *Educational Research* 14, 231-5. *17, 49, 52, 83, 87,93*

Beez, W. V. (1968) 'Influence of Biased Psychological

Reports on Teacher Behavior and Pupil Performance', *Proceedings* 76th Annual Convention, American Psychological Association, No 3, 605-6. *111*

Bennett, N. (1976) *Teaching Styles and Pupil Progress* (London: Open Books). *15, 17, 26, 35, 46, 47, 54, 58*

Bennett, N., and Entwhistle, N. (1977) 'Rite and Wrong: A Reply to "A Chapter of Errors"', *Educational Research* 19, 217-22. *62*

Berlak, A. C., Berlak, H., Bagenstos, N. T., and Mikel, E. R. (1975) 'Teaching and Learning in English Primary Schools', *School Review* 83, 215-43. *47*

Blackie, J. (1967) *Inside the Primary School* (London: H.M.S.O.). *29*

Boydell, D. (1974) 'Teacher-Pupil Contact in Junior Classrooms', *British Journal of Educational Psychology* 44, 313-8. *74, 100*

Boydell, D. (1975) 'Pupil Behaviour in Junior Classrooms', *British Journal of Educational Psychology* 45, 122-9. *94, 99, 101*

Brandis, W., and Bernstein, B. (1974) *Selection and Control: Teachers' Ratings of Children in the Infant School* (London: Routledge and Kegan Paul). *120*

Brandt, R. M. (1975) 'An Observational Portrait of a British Infant School', in Spodek and Walberg 1975 (eds), 101-25. *68*

Brophy, J. E., and Good, T. L. (1970) 'Teachers' Communication of Differential Expectations for Children's Classroom Performance: Some Behavioral Data', *Journal of Educational Psychology* 61, 365-74. *112, 114*

Brown, M., and Precious, N. (1968) *The Integrated Day in the Primary School* (London: Ward Lock Educational). *13, 29, 50*

Bullock Report (1975) *A Language for Life* (London: H.M.S.O.). *15, 26*

Burstall, C. (1970) 'French in the Primary School: Some Early Findings', *Journal of Curriculum Studies* 2, 48-58. *119*

Bussis, A. M., and Chittenden, E. A. (1970) *Analysis of an Approach to Open Education* Interim Report (mimeo) (Princeton, N.J.: E.T.S.). *28*

Cameron-Jones, M., and **Reid, J. F.** (1972) 'Styles of Teaching Reading', *Reading* **6**, 14-20. *71*

Davies, F. R., and **Ashton, P. M. E.** (1975) 'Two Analyses of Teachers' Discussions of Aims in Primary Education', in Taylor 1975 (ed) 15-45. *32*

Dearden, R. F. (1968) *The Philosophy of Primary Education — An Introduction* (London: Routledge and Kegan Paul). *25*

Dearden, R. (1969) 'The Aims of Primary Education', in Peters 1969 (ed), 21-41. *37*

Dearden, R. (1971) 'What is the Integrated Day?', in Walton 1971 (ed), 45-56. *50, 51*

Deutsch, M. (1949) 'An Experimental Study of the Effects of Co-operation and Competition upon Group Process', *Human Relations* **2**, 199-231. *97*

Duthie, J. H. (1970) *Primary School Survey: A Study of the Teacher's Day* (Edinburgh: H.M.S.O.). *81*

Elkin, L. (1964) 'The Behavioural Use of Space by Children', Unpublished manuscript quoted by Sommer 1969. *97*

Featherstone, J. (1967) 'The Primary School Revolution in Britain', Reprint of articles which first appeared 10 August, 2 September, 9 September 1967 in *The New Republic* (New York: Pitman/New Republic). *29*

Garner, J., and **Bing, M.** (1973) 'Inequalities of Teacher-Pupil Contacts', *British Journal of Educational Psychology* **43**, 234-43. *7, 68, 70, 76*

Good, T. L., Biddle, B. J., and **Brophy, J. E.** (1975) *Teachers Make a Difference* (New York: Holt, Rinehart and Winston). *105*

Goodacre, E. J. (1968) *Teachers and their Pupils' Home Background* (Slough: N.F.E.R.). *119*

Gordon, E. M., and **Thomas, A.** (1967) 'Children's Behavioral Style and the Teacher's Appraisal of their Intelligence', *Journal of School Psychology* **5**, 292-300. *115*

Gray, J., and **Satterly, D.** (1976) 'A Chapter of Errors: Teaching Styles and Pupil Progress in Retrospect', *Educational Research* **19**, 45-56. *62*

Grieger, R. M. (1971) 'Pygmalion Revisited: A Loud Call for Caution', *Interchange* 2, 78-90. *113*

Hamilton, D. (1977) *In Search of Structure* (London: Hodder and Stoughton). *88*

Harlen, W., Darwin, A., and **Murphy, M.** (1977) *Match and Mismatch — Raising Questions, Match and Mismatch — Raising Questions: Leader's Guide, Match and Mismatch — Finding Answers* (Edinburgh: Oliver and Boyd for the Schools Council). *40*

Hilsum, S., and **Cane, B. S.** (1971) *The Teacher's Day* (Slough: N.F.E.R.) *15, 46*

Hirst, P. H., and **Peters, R. S.** (1970) *The Logic of Education* (London: Routledge and Kegan Paul). *37*

James, J. (1951) 'A Preliminary Study of the Size Determinant in Small Group Interaction', *American Sociological Review* 16, 474-7. *93*

Kelley, H. H. (1950) 'The Warm-Cold Variable in First Impressions of Persons', *Journal of Personality* 18, 431-9. *107*

Montessori, M. (1965) *Spontaneous Activity in Education* (New York: Schocken Books). *86*

Moran, P. R. (1971) 'The Integrated Day', *Educational Research* 14, 65-9. *51*

Nash, R. (1973) *Classrooms Observed* (London: Routledge and Kegan Paul). *120*

Nash, R. (1976) *Teacher Expectations and Pupil Learning* (London: Routledge and Kegan Paul). *125*

Norum, G. A., Russo, N. J., and **Sommer, R.** (1967) 'Seating Patterns and Group Task', *Psychology in the Schools* 4, 276-80. *97*

Palardy, J. M. (1969) 'What Teachers Believe — What Children Achieve', *Elementary School Journal* 69, 370-4. *110*

Peters, R. S. (1969) (ed) *Perspectives on Plowden* (London: Routledge and Kegan Paul)

Pidgeon, D. A. (1970) *Expectation and Pupil Performance* (Slough: N.F.E.R.). *104*

Plowden, B. (1973) 'Aims in Primary Education', *Education 3-13* 1, 89-90. *9*

Plowden Report (1967) Central Advisory Council for Education (England) *Children and their Primary Schools* Volume 1 Report, Volume 2 Research and Surveys (London: H.M.S.O.). *2, 13, 17, 18, 25, 26-7, 29, 30, 31, 35, 39, 49, 50, 51, 62, 66, 83, 84, 87, 89, 90, 91, 92, 93, 96, 100*

Resnick, L. B. (1972) 'Teacher Behaviour in the Informal Classroom', *Journal of Curriculum Studies* 4, 99-109. *68*

Ridgway, L., and **Lawton, I.** (1968) *Family Grouping in the Primary School* 2nd ed. (London: Ward Lock Educational). *48*

Rist, R. C. (1970) 'Student Social Class and Teacher Expectations: The Self-fulfilling Prophecy in Ghetto Education', *Harvard Educational Review* 40, 411-451. *115*

Rolfe, H. C. (1961) 'Observable Differences in Space Use of Learning Situations in Small and Large Classrooms', Ph.D. thesis, University of California at Berkeley, quoted by Sommer 1969, 103. *89*

Rosen, C., and **Rosen, H.** (1973) *The Language of Primary School Children* (Harmondsworth: Penguin Books, for the Schools Council). *78*

Rosenthal, R., and **Jacobson, L.** (1968) *Pygmalion in the Classroom: Teacher Expectation and Pupils' Intellectual Development* (New York: Holt, Rinehart and Winston). *20, 107*

Sharp, R., and **Green, A.**, with the assistance of **Lewis, J.** (1975) *Education and Social Control: A Study in Progressive Primary Education* (London: Routledge and Kegan Paul). *124*

Snow, R. (1969) 'Unfinished Pygmalion', *Contemporary Psychology* 14, 197-9. *110*

Sommer, R. (1969) *Personal Space: The Behavioral Basis of Design* (Englewood Cliffs, N.J.: Prentice-Hall). *85, 89, 97*

Spodek, B., and **Walberg, H. J.** (1975) (eds) *Studies in Open Education* (New York: Agathon Press)

Taylor, P. H. (1975) (ed) *Aims, Influence and Change in the Primary School Curriculum* (Slough: N.F.E.R.)

Taylor, P. H. and **Holley, B. J.** (1975) 'A Study of the Emphasis Given by Teachers of Different Age Groups to Aims in Primary Education', in Taylor, P. H. 1975 (ed) 46-71. *37*

Taylor, P. H., Reid, W. A., Holley, B. J., and **Exon, G.** (1974) *Purpose, Power and Constraint in the Primary School Curriculum* (London: Macmillan Education). *41, 43, 123*

Thorndike, R. L. (1968) 'Review of "Pygmalion in the Classroom" by Rosenthal and Jacobson', *American Educational Research Association Journal* 5, 708-11. *109, 110*

The Times (1976) 'Progress is not Progressive', 26 April. *58*

Tough, J. (1975) 'Language in Open Education', *Education 3-13* 3, 19-23. *77, 78*

Walberg, H. J., and **Thomas, S. C.** (1971) 'Characteristics of Open Education: Toward an Operational Definition', Report to U.S. Office of Education Title IV Program Contract No OEC-1-7-062805-3936. *29*

Walton, J. (1971) (ed) *The Integrated Day in Theory and Practice* (London: Ward Lock Educational)

Westby-Gibson, D. (1972) (ed) *Education in a Dynamic Society: A Contemporary Sourcebook* (Reading, Mass.: Addison-Wesley)

Withall, J. (1956) 'An Objective Measurement of a Teacher's Classroom Interactions', *Journal of Educational Psychology* 47, 203-212. *69*

Worthington, F. (1969) 'The Observational Study of Classroom Groups', *Forum* 11, 94-6. *98*

Subject index

132